Maynooth Research Guides for Irish Local History

IN THIS SERIES

1 Raymond Refaussé, *Church of Ireland Records*
2 Terry Dooley, *Sources for the History of Landed estates in Ireland*
3 Patrick J. Corish and David Sheehy, *Records of the Catholic Church in Ireland*
4 Jacinta Prunty, *Maps and Mapmaking in Local History*

Maynooth Studies in Irish Local History

IN THIS SERIES

1 Paul Connell, *Parson, Priest and Master: National Education in Co. Meath 1824–41*

2 Denis A. Cronin, *A Galway Gentleman in the Age of Improvement: Robert French of Monivea, 1716–79*

3 Brian Ó Dálaigh, *Ennis in the 18th Century: Portrait of an Urban Community*

4 Séamas Ó Maitiú, *The Humours of Donnybrook: Dublin's Famous Fair and its Suppression*

5 David Broderick, *An Early Toll-Road: The Dublin–Dunleer Turnpike, 1731–1855*

6 John Crawford, *St Catherine's Parish, Dublin 1840–1900: Portrait of a Church of Ireland Community*

7 William Gacquin, *Roscommon Before the Famine: The Parishes of Kiltoom and Cam, 1749–1845*

8 Francis Kelly, *Window on a Catholic Parish: St Mary's Granard, Co. Longford, 1933–68*

9 Charles V. Smith, *Dalkey: Society and Economy in a Small Medieval Irish Town*

10 Desmond J. O'Dowd, *Changing Times: Religion and Society in Nineteenth-Century Celbridge*

11 Proinnsíos Ó Duigneáin, *The Priest and the Protestant Woman*

12 Thomas King, *Carlow: the manor and town, 1674–1721*

13 Joseph Byrne, *War and Peace: The Survival of the Talbots of Malahide 1641–1671*

14 Bob Cullen, *Thomas L. Synnott: The Career of a Dublin Catholic 1830–70*

15 Helen Sheil, *Falling into Wretchedness: Ferbane in the late 1830s*

Maynooth Studies in Irish Local History (cont.)

SOURCES FOR THE HISTORY OF LANDED
ESTATES IN IRELAND

Maynooth Research Guides for Irish Local History

GENERAL EDITOR   Mary Ann Lyons

This pamphlet is one of three in the newly instituted Maynooth Guides for Local History series. Written by specialists in the relevant fields, these volumes are designed to provide historians, and specifically those interested in local history, with practical advice regarding the consultation of specific collections of historical material, thereby enabling them to conduct independent research in a competent and thorough manner. In each volume, a brief history of the relevant institutions is provided and the principal primary sources are identified and critically evaluated, with specific reference to their usefulness to the local historian. Readers receive step by step guidance as to how to conduct their research and are alerted to some of the problems which they might encounter in working with particular collections. Possible avenues for research are suggested and relevant secondary works are also recommended.

I wish to acknowledge the support and interest in this series shown by Dr John Logan, University of Limerick and the valuable input of Dr Raymond Gillespie, N.U.I. Maynooth and Dr Jimmy Kelly, St Patrick's College, Drumcondra.

Maynooth Research Guides for Irish Local History: Number 2

Sources for the History of Landed Estates in Ireland

Terence A.M. Dooley

IRISH ACADEMIC PRESS
DUBLIN • PORTLAND, OR

First published in 2000 by
IRISH ACADEMIC PRESS
44, Northumberland Road, Dublin 4, Ireland
and in the United States of America by
IRISH ACADEMIC PRESS
c/o ISBS, 5804 NE Hassalo Street, Portland, OR 97213–3644.

website: www.iap.ie

British Library Cataloguing in Publication Data
Dooley, Terry
    Sources for the history of landed estates in Ireland. – (Maynooth guides for local
history research)
    1. Land tenure – Ireland – History – Sources
    I. Title
    929.3'415

    ISBN 0–7165–2697–2

Library of Congress Cataloging-in-Publication Data
Dooley, Terry, 1964–
        Sources for the history of landed estates in Ireland / Terry Dooley.
            p.   cm. — (Maynooth guides for local history research)
        Includes bibliographical references and index.
        ISBN 0–7165–2697–2 (pbk)
            1. Ireland—History, Local—Sources. 2. Administration of estates—Ireland—
History—Sources. 3. Landlord and tenant—Ireland—History—Sources.
4. Land tenure—Ireland—History—Sources. I. Title. II. Series.

DA905.D57 2000
941.5—dc21   00–024319

Typeset in 10 pt on 12 pt Bembo by
Carrigboy Typesetting Services, County Cork
Printed by ColourBooks Ltd, Dublin

Contents

List of illustrations

Acknowledgements

In preparing this work the staffs of the following libraries and repositories were enormously helpful and I am most grateful to them: the National Library of Ireland, the Public Record Office Northern Ireland, the National Archives, the Valuation Office, Dublin the Representative Church Body Library, the Russell Library Maynooth, the Registry of Deeds, the Offaly Archaeological and Historical Society, and the Irish Land Commission Office.

I owe thanks to Professor R.V. Comerford for reading a first draft of this work and offering some valuable comments. I am very grateful to Dr Raymond Gillespie and Dr Mary Ann Lyons for entrusting this project to me. Indeed, I owe particular thanks to Dr Lyons for her excellent copy-editing which saved me from many errors.

I wish to thank my family particularly my wife, Annette, and my parents for their continuing support. Finally, I would like to dedicate this work to my son, Conor, who has made the future even more exciting for me than the historical past.

TERENCE A.M. DOOLEY

Introduction

According to Raymond Gillespie and Gerard Moran: 'Local history is the groundwork fundamental to our understanding of the country as a whole.'[1] In the same way the study of local landed estates is fundamental to our understanding of landlordism as a whole. In the past, few detailed studies of local estates were undertaken by historians. This was largely responsible for the credence that was given to a set of generalisations propounded right up to the 1970s that landlords were generally predatory rackrenters who evicted impoverished tenants at the drop of a hat.[2] Since the 1970s, a number of important studies of local estates have appeared that have shown the need to reassess this traditional perception.[3] These have been greatly augmented by more recent national studies which, taken together, have illustrated the complexities involved in the study of Irish landlordism.[4]

It is probably fair to state that the studies of earlier historians suffered from the unavailability of primary source material such as landed estate records. Certainly since the publication of Pomfret's *The struggle for land in Ireland, 1800–1923* in 1930, estate records have become more widely available. These records have proved invaluable in enlightening a new generation of historians as regards what actually occurred on estates in terms of rent increases, estate improvements, and evictions. They have, for example, contributed to a greater degree of accuracy in assessing rent movements and shown that the threat of eviction as a perceived means of effective estate management greatly exceeded actual evictions. Recent findings by historians such as W.E. Vaughan and J.S. Donnelly jr. have much of their basis in estate records which has helped them to reassess the type of information contained in parliamentary papers and pamphlets, the type of sources used by Pomfret. Their work in turn has provided a useful new perspective on landlordism in Ireland in the nineteenth century. Furthermore, Donnelly's pioneering study of County Cork illustrates not only the importance of using estate records but also the value of undertaking such a study at local level.

While records for some estates may not have survived or may not be available to the public in their entirety, or at all, this should not be regarded as a pretext for avoiding the study of an estate. There are sufficient complimentary sources to compensate for lacunae in the material which is available. The aim of this guide is to introduce the researcher to these sources, how to locate them, and how to assess their strengths and weaknesses.

Before undertaking the study of a local estate, the researcher should have a sufficient working knowledge of national history. He or she ought to be aware of what information is available or has been gathered regarding the history of the landed estate. While each estate was obviously unique, the researcher needs to be aware that there were outside economic, social and political forces at work which impinged upon them all and determined their management policy at various stages. The first aim of section one is to provide a broad outline of the history of the landed estate in Ireland from 1800 to around 1930, investigating outside influences which infringed upon estate life. The second aim is to draw the researcher's attention to some of the most important secondary works which are available on various aspects of estate life. Consulting these will help the researcher to determine whether what was happening on a particular local estate was typical of what was happening elsewhere or whether it was peculiar to that estate.

Section two details the sources available to the researcher. It is not rigidly constructed according to any hierarchy of importance, although the use of estate records is necessarily afforded detailed coverage. The merits and weaknesses of each source are discussed and guidelines are given regarding availability. Section three discusses the questions which can be asked of these sources. As Gillespie and Moran point out: 'Abundance of source material is of little value in increasing our understanding of the past unless we ask the right questions of these sources'.[5] This section also briefly explores the areas of estate life which require further examination by local historians.

Estate ownership and management in nineteenth- and early twentieth-century Ireland

I. PRE-FAMINE IRELAND

Throughout the nineteenth century in Ireland, landownership was the preserve of a privileged minority. In 1804, there were an estimated 8,000 to 10,000 landed proprietors in a population of around 5.4 million people. This minority was almost exclusively protestant with only about 5 per cent of land in catholic hands. This was as a direct result of the confiscations of catholic owned property which had taken place under Cromwell, Charles II and William III in the second half of the seventeenth century and the periodic enforcement of the penal laws during the eighteenth century. However, not all estates were owned by individuals: Trinity College, Dublin, for example, was one of the largest landowners in Ireland, while twelve London companies had been granted lands in Co Londonderry in the early seventeenth century in return for a financial contribution to the crown's scheme for the plantation of Ulster.[1]

Nor were all landlords resident. In 1800, as many as one third of landlords were absentees who lived more or less permanently out of the country.[2] Because of their involvement in parliamentary politics, the armed forces, or the civil service, some landlords were by necessity absent from their estates for prolonged periods. By the early 1870s, 46 per cent of estates had resident landlords; 25 per cent had landlords resident elsewhere in Ireland; and 23 per cent were owned either by public institutions or absentees.[3] However, absenteeism was not necessarily synonymous with poor estate management; some of the best-managed estates, such as those of the duke of Devonshire in Cork and Waterford, were owned by absentees.[4]

On absentee estates a great deal depended upon the efficiency of the estate agent. In general, the employment of agents (except in the case of smaller estates managed by their owners) was the most common form of estate management in nineteenth century-Ireland. Some of the greater estates employed a number of sub-agents supervised by the chief agent who, in turn, was accountable to the landlord himself. Agents were responsible for collecting rents (which were usually collected twice a year on appointed gale days in May and November and often in local hotels or estate offices in nearby towns) as well as eliminating arrears; keeping accounts; drawing up leases and ensuring that their covenants were adhered to by tenants; choosing new tenants; supervising estate expenditure; overseeing improvements; carrying out evictions; and valuing property. They often had to arrange loans on behalf of their employer and seek abatements of interest on existing loans. They had to liaise between landlords and tenants, receiving petitions from tenants particularly for reductions of rent.[5] Land agents were responsible for all aspects of estate administration and in the final analysis for managing all the income and expenditure on estates in their charge.[6]

Besides his estate duties, an agent often served as resident magistrate, represented his employer at poor law guardian meetings or on grand juries and organised voters at elections. Because of the importance of these functions and the moderate financial rewards on offer (an agent's normal income was 5 per cent of rents collected but a fixed salary of £800 to £1,000 per annum from single estates was not unknown), the profession attracted younger sons of landlords throughout the nineteenth century. Agents were often local solicitors retired army officers, or wealthy gentlemen.

Other more routine administrative duties on an estate were carried out by bailiffs, stewards and agriculturalists. Larger estates sometimes employed surveyors and valuators although individual landlords and their agents often carried out these duties themselves. The day to day running of an estate office, where established, was the duty of an accountant. Large estates also employed a number of clerks. Landowners such as Lord Devonshire or Lord Ormonde employed an auditor to oversee accounts and a law agent to execute all legal transactions including the preparation of leases and notices to quit. It is because of the input of these various professionals that the collections of surviving estate records belonging to large landowners have been so comprehensive.

The typical Irish estate was centred on the big house, the landlord's country residence, which symbolised his economic strength and social standing in the community. It was surrounded by the demesne which, on average, accounted for about ten per cent of a landlord's total landholding. The demesne usually included a home farm which allowed the big house to be self-sufficient; a kitchen garden to service the family's needs; gardens and lawns for ornamentation and leisure purposes; woodland for the rearing of game; parkland for the grazing of cattle; and a wide variety of outoffices for the housing of animals and for the use of demesne employees such as gardeners, masons and carpenters.

Estates varied greatly in size from the smallest at around 500 acres to those of landed magnates such as the Marquis Conyngham who owned almost 157,000 acres in Meath, Clare and Donegal in the late nineteenth century. Smaller estates were typically concentrated in one county. There were, however, quite a few large estates of over 20,000 acres also concentrated in one county such as the Clonbrock estate in Co Galway. More often large estates were distributed throughout two or more counties.

While at the beginning of the nineteenth century some landlords preferred to deal with their tenants directly, most dealt with middlemen who effectively became intermediate landlords by leasing from the head landlord and renting to sub-tenants.[7] Middlemen usually held large tracts of land from 100 to 1,000 acres and upwards. In the eighteenth century they sometimes held leases for ninety-nine years or more but usually for two or three lives of young persons named in the leases. By the beginning of the nineteenth century new leases tended to be for shorter periods of one life or for twenty-one or thirty-one years. Landlords perceived the middleman system to be a convenient means of relieving them from the troublesome collection of rents from a mass of tenants. However, because of this system not only did sub-letting and sub-division become a way of life in rural Ireland, but long leases prevented landlords from increasing their rents from 1750 to 1815, a period characterised by a steep rise in agricultural prices.[8] Furthermore, middlemen concerned with increasing their own profits showed little enthusiasm for investing in permanent improvements such as new dwelling houses, farm offices or drainage schemes. Indeed, it was the case that landlords, in general, contributed little to improvements in the early nineteenth century. Landlords were unlikely to do so as long as the middleman system prevented them from recouping a return on their investments in the form of higher rents.[9]

Largely because the middleman system had prevented many landlords from realising the full rental potential of their estates, landlords became more reluctant to renew their leases after 1815. They and their agents became more concerned with trying to curb sub-division and sub-letting in favour of the consolidation of holdings. From the 1830s, more stringent management policies were put in place on many estates as landlords tried to correct the errors of their predecessors who had allowed arrears to accumulate, their property to become hopelessly fragmented, their tenantry to slide into abject poverty, and their own indebtedness to grow.

However, there were obstacles to be overcome, not least of which were the frequent outbreaks of agrarian agitation during the first three decades of the nineteenth century. The growth in agrarian unrest coincided with a rapid demographic expansion which saw the population of Ireland increase from 2.5 million in the early 1750s to 8.2 million by the time of the 1841 census.[10] This population growth was most heavily concentrated at the lower end of the rural class structure. J.J. Lee has calculated that cottiers (holders of less than five acres), small farmers (holders of between five and fifteen acres) and agricultural labourers were four times more numerous than large farmers (holders of more than fifteen acres) on the eve of the Famine. In turn, the demand for land ensured that the level of rents was higher than was warranted by agricultural prices. The fall in grain prices in the years after the Napoleonic wars provoked major agrarian disturbances in 1813–16, 1819–22 and in the early 1830s. In each of these outbreaks, the issue of tithes figured prominently.

Tithes were taxes imposed on all landholders, regardless of their denomination, to support the Church of Ireland clergy. From 1735 to 1823, livestock and livestock products had been exempt from liability to tithes. As Irish agriculture was largely pastoral, payments of tithes in this period provoked no great opposition as the burden fell largely on those landholders engaged in tillage. However, the increase in population and a greater demand for corn led to a shift from pastoral to tillage farming at the beginning of the nineteenth century. When corn prices fell dramatically after 1815, opposition to tithes by commercial tillage farmers subsequently increased.[11]

Agrarian disturbances were most pronounced in the southern and western counties during the tithe war of the 1830s though the unrest was not solely motivated by dissatisfaction with the payment of tithes. Perceived inequalities in tenurial arrangements also played their part.[12] Localised agrarian societies such as Whiteboys, Molly Maguires and Caravats were particularly active in Munster and produced intense 'class' conflict between cottiers, labourers and small farmers on the one hand and large farmers (who invariably were the formers' landlords because of varying degrees of sub-letting) on the other.[13] Smallholders and cottiers resented the fact that their rents and the price of conacre (land hired by agricultural labourers to grow potatoes to feed their families) had risen in line with the upward trend in agricultural prices in the early nineteenth century, while the rents paid by large leaseholding farmers remained static. In 1838, the government passed an act which converted tithes into a fixed rent-charge and responsibility for payment was transferred from tenant to landlord. Tithe ceased to be a grievance amongst tenant farmers but it meant that still more money obligations were placed on landlords.

It remains to be seen how the agrarian outbreaks affected estate management in pre-Famine Ireland as it is an area that has still to be explored in depth by historians. Probably more detrimental to landlordism was the growth of indebtedness that characterised the pre-Famine period. The role of spendthrift landlords has tended to be exaggerated in this development, particularly in works of fiction such as Maria Edgeworth's *Castle Rackrent*, yet it cannot be denied that spendthrifts did exist and some landlords spent lavishly on the building of palatial mansions at this time. The earl of Kingston, for example, spent £220,000 on the building of Mitchelstown castle during the 1820s. The early part of the nineteenth century was characterised by a high degree of landlord borrowing as landowners struggled to meet the expense of building big houses, renovating or modifying existing ones or simply maintaining the lifestyle of their predecessors. W.A. Maguire, who has scrutinised the vast collection of Downshire papers, has found that Lord Downshire borrowed £185,500 between 1810 and 1840. Landlords who borrowed during the Napoleonic wars when interest rates were high found it increasingly difficult to meet interest repayments in the years which followed as economic depression set in and small arable farmers fell behind in rental payments. In the 1820s many landlords found themselves forced to grant temporary rental reductions (or abatements) of 25 per cent to their struggling tenants.[14] As was characteristic of economic crises throughout the century, landlords found their arrears accumulated at the same time as their charges remained consistently high.[15] In fact, estate outgoings rose further as a result of the introduction of the system of poor relief in Ireland in 1838. Relief was financed out of local rates, a tax which was levied on occupiers of land. Landlord indebtedness, therefore, was not just a consequence of the Famine: as early as 1844 1,322 estates with a combined rental of £904,000, the properties of bankrupt landowners, were under the control of the Courts of Chancery and Exchequer.

II. THE GREAT FAMINE

The Famine had a number of consequences for landlords and estates. It increased landlord indebtedness: again rents were difficult to collect from 1845 to around 1853 while estate charges remained constant pushing a great number of already heavily burdened landlords nearer to bankruptcy. Other landlords impoverished themselves by helping their destitute tenants through famine relief employment schemes. All were faced with meeting increased charges for poor rates as from August 1843 landlords became liable for all the rates of holdings valued at £4 or less whereas in the past they had shared this burden equally with their tenants. When such occupiers stopped paying their rents, landlords evicted them. Between 1846 and 1853, there were an estimated 70,000 families evicted. These evictions allowed landlords to consolidate holdings on their estates on an extensive scale.[16]

The Famine also brought about a dramatic clearance of bankrupt landlords through reactionary legislation. These landlords, already heavily indebted or encumbranced before the Famine, were unable to survive the sharp fall in rental income and the steep rise in expenditure. By 1849 there was property with an estimated rental of £2 million (out of a total rental of around £13 million) under the control of the Courts of Equity.[17]

The Encumbered Estates Act of 1849 was designed to simplify the transfer of encumbered property by conferring on the purchaser a parliamentary or indefeasible title.[18] Under the auspices of a newly-established Encumbered Estates Court[19], an estate could not be sold without the permission of the landlord if it was not in receivership, or if its level of debts did not exceed half of its annual income. The court could oversee the sale of estates held in fee, leaseholds in perpetuity, or viable leases which had up to sixty years to run. Within a year 1,200 petitions for sale of estates had been lodged with the court, many of which had been brought to insolvency by the effects of the Famine.[20] Over the next thirty years an estimated 25 per cent (or five million acres) changed hands, the biggest transfers taking place in the early 1850s.[21]

Unfortunately for landowners who sold their estates under the act, the market value of land was at rock bottom. While landed property had sold in Ireland for an average of twenty to twenty-five years' purchase of current rents in the 1830s, prices realised in the 1850s were as low as ten to fifteen years' purchase.[22] On the other hand, the traditional view that new proprietors were mainly businessmen now seems largely erroneous. It would appear, in fact, that the wealthier landlords who had survived the Famine bought up at least as much property as urban speculators.

III. POST-FAMINE IRELAND

By the early 1850s, the Irish economy was beginning to recover from the effects of the Famine. Irish agricultural output and prices were rising. Rents were again being paid in full and on time and, indeed, arrears that had in many cases accumulated during the Famine were being cleared. Except for a temporary interruption in the early-1860s this economic prosperity continued until the late 1870s.[23] Many of the country's insolvent landlords had been replaced by new proprietors. Assuming that the smallest estate entitling its owner to be considered a landlord was 500 acres, there were about 6,500 landlords in Ireland by the 1870s. However, most of the country was covered by estates which were much larger than 500 acres.

Agents continued to manage estates in the post-Famine period. Even though in the 1870s a high proportion of agents were still drawn from landed families, there was a tendency to appoint lawyers and solicitors to vacant positions. Land agency firms grew in popularity whereby several estates were administered from one central office in cities such as Dublin and Cork. By 1880, the firm of Hussey and Townsend, for example, collected £250,000 in annual rents from eighty-eight estates in the south of Ireland.[24]

The Famine had done much to end the middleman system. After the Famine, the management of estates became much more vigorous as landlords attempted to make a recovery by ensuring that rents were paid in full and on time and they attempted to oust those middlemen who remained. They actively opposed subdivision and subletting. Small and scattered holdings were consolidated into larger, more compact units. The windfall years of the mid-1850s encouraged a conversion from tillage to pasture farming. Landlords retained large tracts of vacated untenanted land for themselves as they branched more and more into farming to share in what was becoming an increasingly lucrative form of enterprise from the mid-1850s. By the 1870s around 15 per cent of Irish land was held in demesne farms.[25]

However, the overall investment behaviour of landlords in their estates continued to leave a lot to be desired. Cormac Ó Gráda suggests that landlords spent no more than 3 to 5 per cent of their annual rental income on improvements from 1850 to 1875.[26] Yet, despite the unsatisfactory policy of landlords in this area in the post-Famine period, it is fair to conclude that their efforts were still significantly greater than Land League rhetoric would later claim.

Evictions waned in a climate of prosperity which was much freer from agrarian outrage than had been the case in the decades before the Famine.[27] There were very few clearances after 1853, the year which marked the end of the Famine crisis.[28] Evictions continued to be frequent only when arrears were high and agricultural output was low as in the early 1850s, early 1860s, late 1870s and early 1880s. As with evictions, increases in agrarian crime between the Famine and the land war coincided with agricultural crises: the most serious outbreaks occurred in the early 1850s, the early 1860s, the late 1870s and the early 1880s.[29]

Another significant change in estate management in the post-Famine period was the growing reluctance of landlords to grant long leases. Short leases were sometimes granted to occupying tenants which contained husbandry covenants to promote agricultural improvements but by 1870 only about 20 per cent of 662,000 holdings were held on leases, most of them for terms of twenty-one or thirty-one years.[30] The remaining tenants held their land from year to year. Such a tenancy did not expire at the end of each year: the law presumed it continued unchanged from year to year unless surrendered by the tenant. If a landlord wanted to change it he could only do so by litigation and he could not evict a tenant except by due legal process having given six months notice to quit.[31]

After the passage of the 1870 Land Act, there was an increase in the number of leases issued by landlords: about 75,000 were issued in the decade following the act. The act set out to introduce the so-called 'Ulster Custom' throughout the whole of Ireland. The 'Ulster Custom', or tenant right, had as its basis the 'three Fs' – fixity of tenure, fair rent and free sale. The custom, which had no foundation in law but was rather based on the voluntary co-operation of landlords and agents with their tenants, assumed that tenants would not be evicted as long as they paid their rents, which were presumed to be fair, and that they could sell their right in their holding when giving it up. While it was traditionally believed to have existed mainly in Ulster, there is evidence to suggest that something akin to it also existed on southern estates before 1870.[32]

From a landlord's point of view one of the most contentious clauses of the 1870 Land Act was that which provided that an outgoing tenant had to be compensated for improvements he had made to his holding. Thus many of the leases issued in the 1870s contained covenants to protect landlords against the compensation provision. Some covenants were clearly illegal as they attempted to contract the tenant out of compensation for improvement and consequently, as in the case of the duke of Leinster, caused consternation amongst tenants.[33] Furthermore, the exclusion of 135,392 leaseholders and tenants in arrears from

compensation for disturbance affected the prospects of a significant proportion of tenants. On the other hand, where landlords were unable to induce
tenants to contract themselves out of compensation, they often became more
reluctant than they had been in the past to invest in estate improvements.

In general, the increase in agricultural prosperity from the mid-1850s to
the late 1870s favoured tenants more than their landlords. The primary reason
for this is that rents did not rise in accordance with increases in agricultural
incomes during the period.[34] Landlords usually only increased their rents after
the termination of a lease, the transfer of a holding to a son, the succession of
an heir to the estate, or after the revaluation of an estate. A revaluation of an
estate might only take place every twenty years or so. Recent findings by a
number of historians show that rents on average rose by only 20–30 per cent
from the early 1850s to the late 1870s.[35] It would have taken a rise of 40 per
cent to keep apace of the price increments of the time and to have given
landlords a proportionate share of the increased economic prosperity. Most
tenants, therefore, were not rackrented, nor subjected to ceaseless rent
increases, nor, indeed, capriciously evicted as is borne out by the low level of
evictions, particularly from the mid-1860s to the late 1870s.

IV. THE LAND WAR

From the late 1870s, Irish landlordism was rocked by a series of economic
crises, so much so that within just over half a century landlordism as a way of
life had disappeared in Ireland. The agricultural depression which began in
1877 was different from those which preceded it, not only because it was
more protracted, lasting until 1886, but also because a mass movement, the
Land League, grew in response to it. The causes of the land war and the
growth of the Land League has received a great deal of attention from
historians in recent years.[36] The effects which the land war had on individual
estates has been less well documented. Essentially, the Land League called for
rents to be reduced to Griffith's valuation. This valuation had been carried out
between 1852 and 1865 for the purpose of local taxation and was based on
1849–51 prices which meant that by the late 1870s it was perhaps as much as
33 per cent below the real letting value of land.[37] Comparisons of contemporary rents with Griffith's valuation was a tactical ploy exploited by the Land
League as rents that had risen in the period could be deemed to be rackrents
when compared to the old valuation. The effective propaganda campaign of
the league meant that all landlords were painted with the same rackrenting
brush whether they deserved it or not.

It is easy to understand why tenants would clamour for rents to be reduced
to being in line with Griffith's valuation. It is just as easy to understand why
landlords would oppose calls for reductions. Lord Ormonde, for example,

would have suffered a 24 per cent reduction in rental income from £21,352 to £16,359 on his Kilkenny and Tipperary estates. In general, landlords felt that their levels of indebtedness were such that they could not reduce their rents without bringing ruin to themselves.[38] A myriad of estate expenses, family charges, and interest repayments meant that most landlords were fortunate to have around 20–30 per cent of their gross rental income available to them as disposable income at the best of times. In the early stages of agricultural depression landlords, therefore, held out and demanded payment of traditional rents. By doing so they unwittingly fueled the growth in agrarian agitation. As agitation grew and rent strikes began to proliferate, more and more landlords were forced to grant temporary abatements: a reduced rent was better than no rent at all. Consequently, about 25 per cent of all rents due between 1879 and 1882 were lost.

In the past landlords had resorted to borrowing in order to extricate themselves from financial difficulties. As a result of the prevailing economic climate from the 1850s onwards, Irish land had become safe collateral for lending institutions, individuals financiers and even close friends and relations within the landlord class to lend money to Irish landlords on its strength. By the 1870s, many landlords were devoting between 20–30 per cent of their annual rental incomes to interest repayments. Sustained economic depression, declining rental income and the lowering of rents under the terms of the 1881 Land Act meant that most landlords were unable to meet their interest obligations from the early 1880s.[39] When renewed agricultural depression from the mid-1880s was accompanied by the Plan of Campaign, which was ultimately adopted on over 200 estates, landlords found their rental incomes declining even further.[40] Arrears grew to dangerously high levels. This was true even on well-managed estates. In Ireland arrears amounting to around £2.6 million were erased under the terms of the Arrears of Rent (Ireland) Act of 1882. Landlords received around £815,000 of this sum from funds created by the sale of church property while the remaining £1.81 million were cancelled.[41]

The prevailing economic and socio-political climate led to a sharp decline in the selling value of landed estates from 1879 onwards. Irish land was no longer regarded as safe collateral. Mortgagees panicked during the land war and began to call in their loans as landlords temporarily defaulted, closing all avenues of borrowing to the latter.[42] The only viable option for many landlords at this stage was the sale of their estates and the only available purchasers were their own tenants.

V. THE BREAK-UP OF ESTATES FROM 1881

The Land Act of 1881 was more significant for the way in which it infringed upon previously sacrosanct landlords rights than it was for the transfer of land which took place under its terms. It legalised the 'three Fs' which amounted to a recognition of the dual ownership of land.[43] In its objective of promoting land sales, the act was largely unsuccessful with only 703 tenants taking advantage of its terms between 1881 and 1885. The problem was that the terms neither suited tenants nor landlords: tenants could not raise the necessary one fourth of the purchase price; nor were they willing to meet landlords' asking prices of around twenty-three years' purchase.[44] As the bitter agrarian and political struggle of the time closed the doors of the Irish land market to all bidders except the occupying tenants, there was the inevitable gulf between what the tenants regarded as a fair price and what the landlords required.

The acts which followed during the period 1885 to 1896 were more progressive largely because their terms were more conducive to sale, and, perhaps more significantly, because landlord indebtedness had risen considerably through the 1880s making sales more of a necessity. The 1885 act allowed the tenant to obtain the full purchase price from the Land Commission. The annuity was lowered from 5 to 4 per cent and the repayment period was extended from thirty-five to forty-nine years. The purchase money was to be paid to the landlord in cash. However, one fifth was retained as a guarantee deposit in the event of tenants defaulting on their repayments of annuities. Between 1885 and 1891, almost £10 million was advanced allowing tenants to become purchasers. Many of these sales concerned large landowners who sold small outlying estates representing only a percentage of their total acreage but which allowed them to meet immediate debts. The fee simple of these estates was much more valuable than their mortgagable capacity and, at any rate, as we have already seen, loans were almost impossible to secure at this time.

Sales under the 1891 Land Act followed essentially the same pattern: while many small estates came onto the market, larger landowners continued to sell off parts of their estates and with a few exceptions did not sell large tracts. Landlords were now paid in land stock rather than cash. As land stock was subject to fluctuation it could at times be a disincentive to sell but as stock increased in value more land came onto the market, proving that landlords were more likely to sell if the proper terms were put into place.[45]

In total, the land acts from 1870 to 1896 resulted in the purchase of 73,805 holdings of 2.5 million acres for £24.78 million.[46] This represented only about 10 per cent of Ireland's total acreage. Few landlords were enamoured by the average price of 17.3 years' purchase on rents that was available from 1886 to 1902.[47] But many were willing to sell with the proper incentives.[48] In October 1902, the Irish Landowners Convention[49] adopted a resolution stating that landlords needed to be guaranteed 'a price which invested at 3 per cent [would] yield an income approximately equal to the present net income'.[50]

Landlords were now approaching the stage at which they realised that there needed to be a more consensual approach to the whole land purchase issue. And there was a growing body of what could, perhaps, be termed more pragmatic landlords who were prepared to open negotiations with tenant representatives on the subject. Thus, the Irish Land Conference of 1902–03 was established in an attempt to bridge the gulf between what landlords would accept and what tenants would offer. Its report, published in January 1903, provided much of the basis for the act framed by George Wyndham (chief secretary 1900–05) that same year which became the first to make purchase a realistic goal for tenants while simultaneously providing the inducements for landlords to sell. The entire purchase money was, once again, paid in cash to landlords who were also given a 12 per cent bonus on the sale of estates, while tenants were guaranteed that their annuities would be appreciably less than their old rents.[51] Under the Wyndham Act, and the 1909 Land Act, there came about a revolutionary change in land ownership in Ireland.[52] By the end of March 1921, 9,459 estates comprising 270,396 holdings on 9.03 million acres had been sold under these acts for £85.9 million.[53]

There were also significant land sales under the auspices of the Congested Districts Board which had been established under the 1891 Land Act to relieve the problem of congestion especially along the western seaboard.[54] A total of 398 electoral divisions in counties Galway, Leitrim, Mayo, Roscommon, Sligo, Donegal, Kerry and Cork were deemed congested areas. The 1896 Land Act empowered the board to secure advances from the Land Commission for the purchase of estates from landlords instead of having to buy them out of board funds. In 1899, the board purchased the 93,000 acre Dillon estate, with 4,000 tenants and a rental of £20,000 per annum, for £325,000. Of this, £290,000 was paid to the landlord with the remainder being assigned to the redemption of charges and the purchase of tenancy interests. This marked an important stage in the development of the board as the Dillon estate was four times larger than the whole of the seventeen estates purchased by the board up to that point.[55] The 1903 and 1909 Land Acts further extended the powers of the board making more money available and conferring authority upon it to compulsorily acquire land for the relief of congestion. By the time the board was dissolved in 1923 it had purchased 874 estates totalling 1.77 million acres for £8.9 million.[56]

Even the success of the 1903 and 1909 Land Acts did not end landlordism in Ireland. By 1923 over 3,000,000 acres were still in landlord ownership. Some landlords continued to retain huge tracts of tenanted and untenanted land: Lord Farnham in Co Cavan, for example, retained close to 20,000 acres; John Leslie retained over 12,000 acres in Donegal and Monaghan and the earl of Courtown retained almost 13,000 acres in Wexford. Most landlords had retained enough land to finance the upkeep of their big houses. Section three of the 1903 Land Act facilitated hard pressed landlords in retaining their demesnes and other untenanted land in their possession by allowing them to sell such lands to the Land Commission and then to repurchase them, thereby allowing them to retain their standing as substantial farmers.[57] The Land Commission could advance a maximum of £20,000 to each landlord wishing to avail of these terms. During the period 1903–21, landlords repurchased 355 demesnes embracing over 122,000 acres for £1.9 million of which £1.68 million (88 per cent) was advanced by the Land Commission.[58]

Solvency was one possible reason for landlords such as Lord Farnham not selling their estates. There were others such as Lord Clonbrock in Galway who refused to sell because of 'hereditary ties'.[59] And there were landlords such as Lord Cloncurry and Lord Ashtown who had become substantial farmers or graziers and who wanted to continue as such by retaining as much land as that required.[60] Evictions, both during the Famine and at the height of the land war, had led to the creation of large grazing farms from vacated holdings. Landlords held some of these in their own hands; others they let to large graziers. In the post-1881 era, such lettings were frequently arranged on the basis of the 'eleven month system'.[61] This system was exempt from the fair rent fixing terms of the 1881 Land Act and another advantage was that landlords seem to have been able to collect their rents much more easily and punctually from large graziers than they had been from a mass of small tenants.[62]

The grazier system provoked the growth of the United Irish League and the so-called 'ranch war' of the early twentieth century.[63] Many landlords, particularly in the west and in the midlands, who had favoured the grazier system, once again found their estates under prolonged threat from agrarian agitators. In the post-1903 period, the U.I.L. demanded the break-up and distribution of estates belonging to landlords who were not willing to sell under the terms of the Wyndham act. There was prolonged agitation on the Ashtown estate in Co Galway, for example, which lasted from around 1905 to 1914.[64] With the outbreak of World War I agitation temporarily abated on most estates as farming profits improved. Land sales under the land acts were suspended without provoking any great opposition. However, when the war ended and economic prosperity waned, smallholders and the landless once again began to clamour for the break-up of estates.

The Free State land legislation had its roots in a renewed phase of land agitation which erupted, coinciding with the revolutionary period 1919–23.[65] From 1920 tenants on unpurchased estates were as reluctant to meet rental repayments as they had been in the 1880s. Writing in 1922, Patrick Hogan, Minister for Agriculture, claimed that 'for the last couple of years, there had been a general strike by tenants against the payment of rents to landlords. Generally speaking the cause alleged was inability to pay due to the depression in agriculture. Possibly the desire to force land purchase has given its chief strength to this no rent movement'.[66] In April 1923 landlord representatives pointed out that only on about 10–15 per cent of estates were rents paid up to date; on others they were upwards of one and a half years in arrears. Hogan contended that 'while tenants are not paying rents, and while they consider that they need not pay rent in future, they don't want a bill, except on terms which amount to

General Valuation of Ireland.—RETURN OF UNTENANTED LANDS, 1906.

COUNTY OF ANTRIM, RURAL DISTRICT OF AGHALEE.

Electoral Division.	Townland.	Occupier in Valuation Lists.	Area (statute).	Rateable Valuation. Land.	Rateable Valuation. Buildings.	Observations.
			A. R. P.	£ s. d.	£ s. d.	
Aghallon ...	Montiaghs ...	John M. Scott	4 3 35	0 5 0	—	
"	"	John M. Scott	13 0 0	2 15 0	—	
"	"	John M. Scott	11 3 20	2 5 0	—	
"	"	John M Scott	165 3 25	—	—	

COUNTY OF ANTRIM, RURAL DISTRICT OF ANTRIM.

Electoral Division.	Townland.	Occupier in Valuation Lists.	Area (A. R. P.)	Land (£ s. d.)	Buildings (£ s. d.)	Observations.
Antrim (Rural)	Balloo ...	Viscount Massereene and Ferrard	406 0 35	496 0 0	—	
"	"	Viscount Massereene and Ferrard	11 2 27	19 0 0	—	
"	"	Viscount Massereene and Ferrard	29 2 2	28 0 0	—	
"	"	Viscount Massereene and Ferrard	5 1 35	5 10 0	—	
"	"	Viscount Massereene and Ferrard	2 0 0	1 10 0	—	
"	Ballygarnott ...	Viscount Massereene and Ferrard	0 2 35	0 15 0	—	
"	Ballycraigy ...	Robert Thompson	59 . 5	69 5 0	2 15 0	
"	"	Robert Thompson	25 0 32	29 10 0	—	
"	"	Robert Thompson	25 0 35	30 15 0	—	
"	"	Robert Thompson	58 0 10	79 10 0	—	
"	Deerpark ...	Viscount Massereene and Ferrard	624 2 3	557 15 0	—	
"	Muckamore ...	Samuel Thompson	30 2 2	39 10 0	—	
"	Oldstone ...	Reps. James Chaine	1 3 25	1 0 0	—	
"	"	Robert Thompson	62 2 25	75 15 0	—	
"	Park Hall ...	George J. Clarke	22 0 10	30 10 0	—	
"	Townparks ...	Viscount Massereene and Ferrard	2 0 15	2 10 0	—	
"	"	Viscount Massereene and Ferrard	6 2 35	10 0 0	—	
"	"	Viscount Massereene and Ferrard	16 0 30	20 15 0	—	
"	"	Viscount Massereene and Ferrard	62 0 0	95 0 0	65 0 0	Attached to Mansion house.
"	"	Viscount Massereene and Ferrard	5 3 20	13 0 0	—	
"	"	Viscount Massereene and Ferrard	6 0 5	10 0 0	—	
Ballyclare (Rural)	Ballycor ...	William Johnston	3 1 0	1 10 0	—	
Ballynadrentagh	Ballymacmary	Lieut.-Gen. T. H. Pakenham	54 2 35	54 16 0	—	
"	,	Lieut.-Gen. T. H. Pakenham	55 2 30	53 0 0	1 10 0	
"	"	Lieut.-Gen. T. H. Pakenham	22 0 35	23 10 0	8 0 0	
"	Croishill ...	Lieut.-Gen. T. H. Pakenham	8 2 20	6 5 0	—	
"	"	Lieut.-Gen. T. H. Pakenham	14 0 0	7 10 0	—	
"	Gartree ...	Lieut.-Gen. T. H. Pakenham	5?5 3 23	528 0 0	230 0 0	Mansion house.
"	"	Lieut.-Gen. T. H. Pakenham	1 1 20	0 5 0	—	
"	"	Lieut.-Gen. T. H. Pakenham	4 0 5	14 5 0	0 15 0	
"	"	Lieut.-Gen. T. H. Pakenham	5 1 25	6 5 0	—	
"	Gortnagallon ...	Lieut.-Gen. T. H. Pakenham	0 1 10	0 5 0	—	
Cargin ...	Ballynaleney ..	Lord O'Neill	7 2 30	—	—	
"	Ballynamullan	Lord O'Neill	4 3 20	—	—	
"	Carlane ...	Lord O'Neill	0 2 0	—	—	
"	Gallagh ...	Lord O'Neill	3 1 20	—	—	
Connor ...	Carnearney ...	Viscount Massereene and Ferrard	63 0 20	12 10 0	—	
"	Tardree ...	Viscount Massereene and Ferrard	53 3 15	15 0 0	—	
"	"	Viscount Massereene and Ferrard	11 3 30	5 10 0	7 0 0	
"	"	Viscount Massereene and Ferrard	8 3 25	2 10 0	—	
"	Maxwell's Walls	George J. Clarke	5 1 24	—	—	
"	Castlegore ...	Viscount Massereene and Ferrard	29 0 0	9 0 0	—	
Connor ...	Ross ...	Viscount Massereene and Ferrard	3 0 20	1 0 0	—	
Craigarogan	Craigarogan ...	Lieut.-Gen. T. H. Pakenham	14 2 0	5 0 0	—	
Crumlin ...	Ballytromery ...	Lieut.-Gen. T. H. Pakenham	1 0 0	1 0 0	—	
"	Ballygortgarve	Lieut.-Gen. T. H. Pakenham	3 3 0	2 0 0	—	
"	Ballynacrevan...	Lieut.-Gen. T. H. Pakenham	20 0 30	18 0 0	—	
Donegore ...	Ballynoe ...	George J. Clarke	0 1 15	0 5 0	—	
Kilbride ...	Drumadarragh	Thomas J. Dixon	65 2 30	66 10 0	48 0 0	Mansion house.
"	"	Thomas J. Dixon	622 0 10	117 5 0	1 5 0	
"	"	Thomas J. Dixon	23 2 30	19 10 0	1 10 0	
Randalstown ...	Ballygrooby ...	Lord O'Neill	2 1 0	2 10 0	—	
"	"	Lord O'Neill	0 1 20	0 10 0	—	
"	-	Lord O'Neill	3 2 14	4 15 0	34 0 0	
"	Craigmore ...	Lord O'Neill	37 3 10	14 0 0	—	
"	Feehogue ...	Lord O'Neill	11 1 35	11 15 0	—	
"	"	Lord O'Neill	1 1 20	1 5 0	—	
"	"	Lord O'Neill	6 1 19	7 5 0	—	
"	Half Umry ...	Lord O'Neill	87 0 36	45 0 0	—	
"	Kilbegs ...	Lord O'Neill	45 1 0	19 0 0	—	
"	Lurgan West ...	Lord O'Neill	6 0 5	6 0 0	—	
"	"	Lord O'Neill	7 1 25	7 15 0	—	
"	Maghereagh ... (Parish of Drummaul).	Lord O'Neill	27 3 19	—	—	
"	Randalstown ...	Lord O'Neill	3 2 10	3 15 0	—	

A

1. Extract from *Return of untenanted lands in rural districts* ... HC 1906, c.177.

confiscation'.[67] It was largely with confiscation in mind that the terms of the 1923 Land Act were framed.

Under the terms of the 1923 Act all land and also untenanted land situated in congested districts was to be vested in the Land Commission on appointed days to be declared by the Land Commission. There were limited exceptions such as home farms and demesnes.[68] All exceptions, other than public authority or corporation lands, could be disregarded by the Land Commission if it declared any estate to be important in the relief of congestion.

The transfer of tenanted holdings under the 1923 Act was slow and unsatisfactory from the government's point of view and was hampered by legal constraints. The 1931 Land Act was intended to speed up the process. This act enabled the vesting of holdings in the Land Commission to be accomplished by means of the gazetting of lists of vested holdings in the *Iris Oifigiúil*, subject to the correction of errors and omissions that might be found necessary. Every tenant of a holding included in the published list was deemed to have entered into an agreement for the purchase of his holding on the appointed day at the standard price. However, loopholes continued to be exploited. Frank Aiken, speaking in the Dáil in July 1933 on the new land bill of that year, summarised these difficulties. Aiken claimed that 'very few realise the legal and other difficulties which the Land Commission have to surmount before they can divide even a single estate' and that 'the safeguards given to home farms and demesne lands have operated to impede the work of the Land Commission in the relief of congestion'.[69] Moreover there were lengthy procedures which led to administrative difficulties.

The 1933 Land Act empowered the Land Commission to redistribute any property it found suitable with the exception of ordinary owner-occupied farms. This prevented landowners from laying claim to outlying farms as they had done in the past for it empowered the Land Commission to acquire property of landowners who did not reside in its immediate vicinity or who did not use this property 'in the same manner as an ordinary farmer in accordance with proper methods of husbandry'.[70] Practically all agricultural lands were, therefore, bought out from former landlords. By the late 1930s the Free State land acts had succeeded in transferring 3.1 million acres, embracing 113,800 holdings, for £20.8 million.[71] The largest estates vested in the Land Commission from 1923 to the mid-1930s included, for example, over 11,000 acres of the marquis of Waterford; almost 12,000 acres of Viscount Powerscourt in Wicklow; almost 11,000 acres of Dame B.F.E. Carew in Tipperary; 11,000 acres of the duke of Devonshire in Waterford; 11,000 acres of Lady Edith Windham in Monaghan; and almost 20,000 acres of Lord Farnham in Cavan.

Primary sources for the study
of a landed estate

INTRODUCTION

The aim of this section is to introduce the reader to the most important primary sources which are available for the study of a landed estate in Ireland. Essentially what is offered is the ideal in that it describes all sources that could be available in the perfect situation. Unfortunately, this ideal is not always attainable. Nonetheless with the variety of sources examined below, the researcher should be able to gain an insight into various aspects of the layout, topography, management, and rise and decline of an individual estate. The discussion which follows analyses the strengths and weaknesses of a range of sources and directs the researcher to the current location of each. The sources are not arranged in any hierarchical order of importance. The survey begins with an overview of works of reference, directories and gazetteers because these help to locate an estate and they often offer a freeze-frame introduction to the area in which it was situated.

I. WORKS OF REFERENCE, DIRECTORIES AND GAZETTEERS

There are a number of works of reference available, particularly for the second half of the nineteenth century, which will enable the local historian to locate the estate being studied (at least on a county basis), to find its acreage and to estimate its valuation. The most important of these are John Bateman, *The great landowners of Great Britain and Ireland* (reprinted with an introduction by David Spring, Leicester, 1971) and U.H. Hussey De Burgh, *The landowners of Ireland: an alphabetical list of the owners of estates of 500 acres or £500 valuation and upwards in Ireland* (Dublin, 1881). These works also offer incidental information on the sitting landlord regarding his education, army career (if any), and the club(s) to which he belonged. Unlike De Burgh, Bateman indicates if landlords with property in Ireland also owned property in Britain.

For the nineteenth century a variety of gazetteers and directories are available which offer some information on landowners in an area. The most useful gazetteer for pre-Famine Ireland is Samuel Lewis, *A topographical dictionary for Ireland* (2 volumes, London, 1837). It is organised on a county basis and parishes within each county are organised in alphabetical order.

Most of the information contained in this gazetteer was supplied by landlords. An overview is given for each county which offers some information on the range in size of estates there or the average size of farm holdings. One is alerted to the variations in agricultural practice within an area or differences in the quality of land, information which may be useful when looking, for example, at the rental capacity of farm holdings.

Details are also recorded in Lewis's *Topographical dictionary* on landlords' houses and demesnes. For example, he described Currah, Co Limerick, home of Sir Aubrey De Vere as an:

> elegant residence situated in the centre of a wide, fertile, undulating demesne, enriched with luxuriant woods and plantations and embellished with a picturesque lake; the mansion is of hewn limestone with a front of beautiful design commanding the lake; there are three entrances to the park, of which the lodge at that from Adare is the most handsome.[1]

Apart from Lewis' *Topographical dictionary* and the three volume *Parliamentary gazetteer of Ireland* published in 1846 there is no other comparable gazetteer available for the later nineteenth century.

Directories such as *Thom's almanac and official directory of the United Kingdom and Ireland* (1845–), *Pigot's City of Dublin and Hibernian Provincial Directory*, and *Slater's National Commercial Directory of Ireland* (published occasionally, 1846–94) are to be found in the National Library of Ireland and other main repositories. Essentially these are collections of information on a wide variety of topics and while they are arguably of more benefit to urban historians, directories do provide some useful, if limited, information on estates. From the mid-1870s, details regarding the size of most estates in Ireland can be found in *Thom's directory*. *Slater's directory* also provides lists of the prominent nobility and gentry families in each area. An indication of local landlord patronage can be gauged from their association with various local schools.[2]

There are other directories in existence that deal specifically with individual counties. These may have been once off or occasional publications. These works can be located by examining the subject volumes of the printed books catalogues in the National Library of Ireland under the name of the county[3] or by consulting the guide to Irish directories produced by Rosemary ffoliott and Donal Begley in 1981 which lists all the Dublin and provincial directories in chronological order.[4]

The beginning of the nineteenth century also saw the publication of a number of important statistical surveys carried out by the Royal Dublin Society, which, like the works above, can provide the historian with at least some information on the topographical, social and economic life of the area in which the estate was located. For example, James McParland's *Statistical survey of Co Mayo, with observations on the means of improvement* (Dublin, 1802) offers a fairly detailed physical description of each of Mayo's nine baronies; farm sizes and agricultural practices in the county; fairs and agricultural prices. It also contains a list of the principal landlords in Mayo at that time, classifying them as resident or absentee. Unfortunately no surveys were carried out for counties Carlow, Fermanagh, Limerick, Kerry, Westmeath, Louth, Longford or Waterford.

Genealogical information on landlords and their families can be found in works such as G.E. Corkayne, *Complete peerage of England, Scotland, Ireland etc., extant, extinct and dormant* (revised edition by Vicary Gibbs and others, 13 volumes, London, 1910–49); Sir Bernard Burke, *Burke's landed gentry of Ireland* (London, various editions); and idem, *Burke's peerage, baronetage and knightage* (London, various editions). Mark Bence-Jones' *A guide to Irish country houses* (revised edition, London, 1988) is a masterful survey of over 2,000 houses of Irish landlords, offering a brief glimpse of their architectural shape and history. Also useful in this respect, particularly for houses on large estates in Ireland at the beginning of the nineteenth century, is J.P. Neale's *Views of the seats of noblemen in England, Wales, and Scotland and Ireland* (London, 1820). For a valuable insight into the practice of estate management, Thomas De Moleyn's *The landlords and agents practical guide* (various editions, Dublin, 1860–77) is a useful starting point.

II. ESTATE RECORDS

The most important sources available to a researcher undertaking the study of a landed estate are contained in its estate records. Since the 1970s, studies by historians such as J.S. Donnelly jr. and W.E. Vaughan have shown the value and, indeed, necessity of using these sources. Estate records reveal the reality of estate life as opposed to the myth which has often been handed down in oral history or, indeed, in biased history texts which perpetuated the stereotype of the rackrenting, capricious and alien landlord.

The first step for the researcher is actually finding out if records survive for an estate and if so where they are located. This can be done in a number of ways. Firstly, one should consult Richard Hayes's *Manuscript sources for the history of Irish civilisation* (Boston, Mass., 1966). For the student of the landed estate the most relevant volumes are numbers 1–4 dealing with persons, and volumes 7–8 dealing with place. In these volumes one should look up the name of the landlord or the name of the area(s) where the estate was located. One will find a brief description of the manuscript, the manuscript number if available in the National Library of Ireland[5] or, if not, the name of the repository where the manuscript is stored.[6] For example, looking under the name of Cloncurry, one finds the following entry: 'MSS 5661–5664: Cloncurry papers: Domestic farm and workmen's accounts relating to Lord Cloncurry's

Manuscript Sources for the History of Irish Civilization—First Supplement

Clonbrock (Robert Dillon, 3rd Baron):

Ms. 19,536 - 19,542: Clonbrook Papers: Cash books of the Clonbrock estates, Co. Galway, 7 volumes, 1 Jan. 1870 - 31 Jul. 1942.

Clonbrock (Robert Dillon, 3rd Baron):

Ms. 19,545: Clonbrook Papers: Expenses book of Robert Dillon, 3rd Baron Clonbrook, Co. Galway in course of journey to Switzerland, 1 volume, Aug.- Sept., 1876.

Clonbrock (Robert Dillon, 3rd Baron):

Ms. 19,546: Clonbrook Papers: Farm account book, Clonbrook, Co. Galway, 1 volume, 1 Jan. 1878-1946.

Clonbrock (Robert Dillon 3rd Baron):

Mss. 19,633-19,645: Clonbrook Papers: Rentals and accounts of the estate of Robert Dillon, 3rd Baron Clonbrook, in Co. Galway, 13 volumes, 1880-1892.

Clonbrock (Robert Dillon, 3rd Baron):

Mss. 19,646-19,651: Clonbrook Papers: Rentals and accounts of the estate of Robert Dillon, 3rd Baron Clonbrook and Luke Gerald Dillon, 4th Baron Clonbrook in Co. Galway, 6 volumes, 1893-1898.

Clonbrock (Robert Edward Dillon, 5th Baron):

Mss. 19,507-19,514: Clonbrook Papers: Estate, farm and household account books of the Clonbrook estates, Co. Galway, 8 large volumes, 1834-1935.

Clonbrock (Robert Edward Dillon, 5th Baron):

Ms. 19,536 - 19,542: Clonbrock Papers: Cash books of the Clonbrock estates, Co. Galway, 7 volumes, 1 Jan. 1870 - 31 Jul. 1942.

Clonbrock (Robert Edward Dillon, 5th Baron):

Ms. 19,546: Clonbrook Papers: Farm account book, Clonbrook, Co. Galway, 1 volume, 1 Jan. 1878 - 1946.

Clonbrock (Robert Edward, 5th Baron):

Ms. 19,563-19,566: Clonbrook Papers: Cellar books at Clonbrook, Co. Galway, 4 vols. 13 Feb. 1898 - 15 Nov. 1902, 29 Dec. 1907 - 11 Mar. 1927.

Clonbrock (Robert Edward Dillon, 5th Baron):

Ms. 19,671: Clonbrook Papers: Album of newscuttings and miscellaneous papers including obituary notices of the 4th and 5th Barons Clonbrook, material re Home Rule question in Co. Galway, World War I, and the Civil War, c. 1911-1926.

Clonbrock (Robert Edward Dillon, 5th Baron):

Ms. 19,574: Clonbrook Papers: Register of motor journeys to and from Clonbrook, Co. Galway, 1 small volume, 1916-1922.

Clonbrock (Robert Edward Dillon, 5th Baron):

Ms. 19,575-19,576: Clonbrook Papers: Pass books of Robert Edward Dillon, 5th Baron Clonbrook, in account with the Bank of Ireland, 2 volumes, 1917-1926.

Clonbrock (Robert Edward Dillon, 5th Baron):

Ms. 19,577: Clonbrook Papers: Cattle and sheep bought and sold book of the estate in Co. Galway of Robert Edward Dillon, 5th Baron Clonbrook and his successors, 1 Jun. 1926-20 May 1942.

Clonbrock Drawing Society:

Ms. 20,993: Miscellaneous items including permit for K.A. Gibbon of Waterford to use car, 1919; printed rules of Clonbrook Drawing Society, 1891.

Clonbrook Papers:

Clonbrook Papers: Papers of the family of Dillon, Lords Clonbrook, of Ahascragh, Co. Galway, consisting of deeds, correspondence, estate papers and accounts, c. 16th - 20th c., including a large amount of material relating to the late 19th and 20th c. Several thousand documents. [Now in National Library of Ireland. Partly sorted].

Clonbrook Papers:

Ms. 19,487: Clonbrook Papers: Account book of Robert Dillon, 1st Baron Clonbrook, Co. Galway, 1 volume, c.1777-1794.

Clonbrook Papers:

Ms. 19,672: Clonbrook Papers: Volume of maps of the estate of Edward Crofton, Esq., in the County of Roscommon, by Charles Frisell, Nov. 1777. 35 coloured maps, mainly 11" x 9", with accompanying lists of tenants' holdings and observations thereon, also rentroll for the estates, May 1778.

Clonbrook Papers:

Ms. 19,488: Clonbrook Papers: Servants' wages book of Robert Dillon, 1st Baron Clonbrook of Co. Galway, 1 volume, c. 1779-1794.

Clonbrook Papers:

Mss. 19,489-19,491: Clonbrook Papers: Expenses books of Robert Dillon, 1st Baron Clonbrook, Co. Galway, 3 small volumes, 1780-1786, 1789-1794.

Clonbrook Papers:

Mss. 19,493-19,498: Clonbrook Papers: Receipts and payments memoranda books of Luke Dillon, 2nd Baron Clonbrook, relating mainly to estates in Cos. Galway and Limerick, 6 small volumes, c. 1796-1808.

Clonbrook Papers:

Ms. 19,492: Clonbrook Papers: Account book of Otway Toler [agent] to Luke Dillon, 2nd Baron Clonbrook, 1 small volume, [1796-1801].

Clonbrook Papers:

Ms. 19,499 - 19,500: Clonbrook Papers: Expenses books of Luke Dillon, 2nd Baron Clonbrook also containing some brief diary entries, 2 small volumes, 1799, 1801.

Clonbrook Papers:

Ms. 19,673: Clonbrook Papers: Small notebook containing sailing instructions for the south of England coast and also a short account of sailing off the Dieppe area of France, early 19th c.

Clonbrook Papers:

Ms. 19,674: Clonbrook Papers: Small volume containing prescriptions for animal ailments, also a recipe for a substitute for wine, early 19th c.

Clonbrook Papers:

Ms. 19,501: Clonbrook Papers: Tenants' ledger of the estate in Cos. Galway, Limerick and Roscommon, of Luke Dillon, 2nd Baron Clonbrook, 1801-1806.

Clonbrook Papers:

Ms. 19,502: Clonbrook Papers: Cash book of Luke Dillon, 2nd Baron Clonbrook, Co. Galway, 1 volume, c. 1804-1818.

Clonbrook Papers:

Ms. 19,503: Clonbrook Papers: Cellar book of Luke Dillon, 2nd Baron Clonbrook and Robert Dillon, 3rd Baron Clonbrook, Co. Galway, 1 small volume, 1808- 1827.

Clonbrook Papers:

Ms. 19,504: Clonbrook Papers: Servants' wages book of Luke Dillon, 2nd Baron Clonbrook, Co. Galway, 1 small volume, 1809-1816.

Clonbrook Papers:

Ms. 19,505: Clonbrook Papers: Expenses book of Luke Dillon, 2nd Baron Clonbrook, Co. Galway 1 small volume, 1812-1826.

Clonbrook Papers:

Ms. 19,506: Clonbrook Papers: Expenses book of Luke Dillon, 2nd Baron Clonbrook, Co. Galway, 1 small volume, 1818-1820.

Clonbrook Papers:

Ms. 22,008 - 22,009: Clonbrook Papers: A survey of the estate of the Right Honble, Lord Clonbrook situate in the County of Galway. By James Vaughan and Sons, Dublin [mainly by Edward Vaughan]. 88 coloured maps in 2 vols. 31" x 20", with accompanying lists of tenants and respective holdings, 1832.

Clonbrook Papers:

Ms. 19,585-19,608: Clonbrook Papers: Rentals and accounts of the estates of Robert Dillon, 3rd Baron Clonbrook, in Cos. Galway and Roscommon, 24 vols., 1827-1840.

Clonbrook Papers:

Ms. 19,515-19,516: Clonbrook Papers: Cellar books of Robert Dillon, 3rd Baron Clonbrook, Co. Galway, 2 volumes, 12 Oct. 1833 - Jul. 1845. 18 Sept. 1845 - 29 Apr. 1851.

Clonbrook Papers:

Mss. 19,507-19,514: Clonbrook Papers: Estate, farm and household account books of the Clonbrook estates, Co. Galway, 8 large volumes, 1834-1935.

Clonbrook Papers:

Ms. 22,010: Clonbrook Papers: Lists of tenants and holdings of the Clonbrook, Ballydonnelan and Castlegar estates in Co. Galway. By Edward Vaughan. 1 vol., 44pp. 27" x 20", 1839. [Index to Ms. 22,008 22,009].

Clonbrook Papers:

Ms. 19,609-19,616: Clonbrook Papers: Rentals and accounts of the estate of Robert Dillon, 3rd Baron Clonbrook, in Cos. Galway, 8 volumes, 1840-1844.

Clonbrook Papers:

Ms. 19,517-19,522: Clonbrook Papers: Pass books of Robert Dillon, 3rd Baron Clonbrook, Co. Galway, in account with the Bank of Ireland, 6 volumes, 1842-1857, 1871-1893.

Clonbrook Papers:

Ms. 19,523-19,527: Clonbrook Papers: Expenses books of Robert Dillon, 3rd Baron Clonbrook and Caroline Lady Clonbrock, 5 small volumes, 1844, 1853, 1858-1860.

Clonbrook Papers:

Ms. 19,528: Clonbrook Papers: Household and general expenses books, Clonbrook, Co. Galway, 3 small volumes, 1846-1864, 1868-1872.

Clonbrook Papers:

Ms. 19,546: Clonbrook Papers: Farm account book, Clonbrook, Co. Galway, 1 volume, 1 Jan. 1878 - 1946.

2. Extract from Richard Hayes, *Manuscript sources for the history of Irish civilisation*, first supplement, vol. i (Dublin, 1979).

estates in Kildare and Limerick, c.1830–1899 (discontinuous, with rentals and accounts 1860–99)'. Also listed are some manuscripts, the originals of which are stored outside the N.L.I., but copies of which may be available in the library on microfilm. These will have a number such as N104 P33 at the end of the entry. Occasionally one may also come across a reference number such as P.C. 4180. 'P.C.' stands for 'packing case' which means that these papers are also stored in the National Library but have not yet been catalogued and are, therefore, not on open access. However, access may in some cases be granted further to having written to the Keeper of Manuscripts in the National Library seeking permission to consult the collection.

In the National Library, the card catalogue in the manuscript reading room should also be consulted as these cards contain information on more recently acquired estate papers not to be found in Hayes's *Manuscript sources*. There are also 'special lists' available on family or estate collections in the National Library which have only recently been sorted. 'Special list A' is an index to these collections. It records the number of the list in which a collection is catalogued and this list can be consulted in the manuscript reading room. One should also consult the periodic reports of the Irish Manuscript Commission and National Library of Ireland on estate collections in private hands, which are likewise available in the National Library. These reports, based on the work of Sir John Ainsworth, provide a summary of the material that was available in private collections around the 1950s. Some of these collections may subsequently have been transferred to various repositories or may even, unfortunately, have been destroyed.

The National Library is, of course, not the only repository which contains a comprehensive collection of Irish estate papers. There is also a very comprehensive collection in the Public Record Office Northern Ireland (P.R.O.N.I.)[7] Information on estate records held there can be found in P.R.O.N.I., *Guide to estate collections* (Belfast, 1994), or on website http://proni.nics.gov.uk/records/landed.htm. The National Archives also houses some estate collections.[8] While no printed guide exists, indexes to them can be found on the shelves in the reading room. Estate collections may also be found in other Irish repositories such as Trinity College Library,[9] or British repositories such as the Public Record Office, London. Information on Irish estate papers housed in various repositories throughout the United Kingdom may be obtained from the National Register of Archives website at http://www.hmc.gov.uk/nra/indexes.htm. Here one can search under personal and family name or place name. Looking under the place name of County Monaghan, for example, one finds twenty-five listings of which eighteen are estate records of landed families in that county. Of these, one finds that estate records of the Shirley family of Lough Fea, for example, are to be found in P.R.O.N.I. and in Warwickshire County Record Office. In order to find the records of peerage families one should enter the peerage title under 'descriptive term' should the records not

No.	DENOMINATIONS	CHARGE			DISCHARGE						
		Arrears	One Year's Rent ending 25 Mar. 1908	Total	Cash Received	Poor Rate Allowed	Income Tax Allowed	Abatement Allowed	Arrear Abandoned	Arrear due	Total
	Brought Forward	387 10 6½	684 3 5	1060 13 11½	445 5 11½	16 13 11½	20 13 2	294 7 4½	696 12 6	4817 19 7	1080 13 11½
37	*Cuttaghan*	11 19 1	519 5 4	531 4 5	429 2 4	4 11 8		10 35 1 6		62 8 1	531 4 5
38	*Lisheenakeeran*	287 10 11	262 17	550 7 11	201 12 3			18 12 4	17 16 7	312 6 9	550 7 11
39	*Rathdrum*		327 6 8	327 6 8	267 14			59 12 8			327 6 8
40	*Spollinstown*	8 17	551 6 8	560 3 5	495 5 5	5 16 2	3 3 4	39 15	2 10 6	13 10	560 3 5
41	*Togher*	258 9 9	150 19	409 8 9	92 18 7			3 8		313 2 2	409 8 9
42	*Tullamoore*	83 3 9	924 5 5	1007 9 2	879 19 1½	9 1 11½	24 10 10½		2 12	91 5 2½	1007 9 2
43	*Factory Farm*		50 18 9	50 18 9	45 17 6			5 13			50 18 9
44	*Tureen*		57 10 2	57 10 2	54 12 8			2 17 6			57 10 2
45	*Wood of O.*	31 14 5	141 15 2	173 9 7	129 13 5		2 1 1	8 10		39 5 1	173 9 7
46	*Mellon Point.*	12	1	13						13	13
	Totals	2451 5 5½	9831 7 4	14482 12 9½	7546 1 3	36 3 9	50 9 3½	467 9	719 12 7	5662 16 11½	14482 12 9½

3. Extract from a rental for the Charleville estate, Tullamore,
County Offaly, for the year ending 31 March 1909
(courtesy of Offaly Historical Society).

appear under family name. It is important to realise that some estate collections
have been scattered amongst a number of repositories. This is particularly true
of those belonging to absentee or semi-absentee landowners who had estates
in Ireland and Britain or, indeed, in different parts of Ireland.

If no records pertaining to a particular estate can be traced to a major
repository, it is worth investigating if an estate's solicitors are still in business as
they may still have family papers or know of their whereabouts.[10] Solicitors
may be able to put the researcher in contact with descendants of the landed
family who may still retain at least some of the estate records in their
possession. Descendants may also be traced by using the most recent editions
of *Burke's landed gentry of Ireland* or *Burke's peerage, baronetage and knightage.*
Finally, local libraries, heritage centres and local archives now house some
estate collections and are also worth contacting.

Having located an estate collection, what can one hope to find in them? It
is perhaps best to answer this question by reference to what one could hope
to find in a complete collection. Estate rentals are particularly valuable
especially when they exist in annual or semi-annual series. They detail rents
due, rents paid, and the extent of arrears, indicating how successful a landlord
was in collecting his rental income. They enable a study of the effects of
periods of crises such as the Famine of the 1840s or the land war of the 1880s

on estate rents. When available in a long unbroken series with uniform headings, rentals allow the researcher to calculate the size of rent increases on individual holdings or on the estate as a whole, and to compare rent increases on individual holdings. In analysing rent movements on an estate, one should consider agricultural incomes as the level of agricultural incomes determined the tenants' capacity to pay the asking rent. A standard form of rental only really became popular in the post-Famine period; prior to that estate records were often kept by agents on loose sheets of paper, which down through the years were much less likely to survive.

The Clonbrock estate in Co Galway was divided into seven administrative units – Doone, Castlegar, Ballydonelan, Dalyston, Luansbury, Lecarrow and Pallas. The rental ledgers for each year are divided according to these seven administrative units. The names of tenants in each estate are listed by the townland in which they lived. Their arrears for the previous two gale days are specified, as are the half year's rent due, the rent and arrears received and the remaining arrears due thereafter. These details are followed by a summary of the rental accounts for each administrative unit giving totals of rents received, rent and arrears due etc. Finally, there is a summary of rental accounts for the estate as a whole.

Rent books were kept by landlords or their agents to keep an account with individual tenants. They record the tenant's name, the gale days on which his rent was due, the amount paid on the last gale day and the amount outstanding in arrears. They may also record any change in tenancies due, for example, to the falling in of leases. Comments columns in such ledgers can be useful. They sometimes record the landlord's or the agent's observations on tenants, offering reasons why a tenant is unable to meet his/her full rental obligation. The comments columns in the Clonbrock rent ledger for 1881, a time when the landlord was having difficulties in collecting rents due to agricultural depression and Land League agitation, shows that individual tenants were 'very poor, unable to pay'; 'wife has lambs to sell, he [her husband] is gone to America to make rent'; or that the tenant was now 'dead. House pulled down' or had been 'ejected. Arrears lost. Land relet'.[11]

There are a number of different types of estate account books. Some comprehensive collections have account books which detail the day to day expenditure on an estate. The Clonbrock estate account books for the second half of the nineteenth century provide a daily record of expenses incurred in the maintenance of the big house, demesne, farm, gardens, stables, and labour. These account books also record any income received including even the sum of £4.3s.11d. received in 1868 for 'dripping' sold from the house.[12] Fortunately, for the researcher interested only in end of year accounts, the collection also contains account books where all expenses are totaled and balanced against all income received. Income was primarily made up of rents received from tenants but accounts show that some landlords received additional income from a variety of other sources as diverse as the selling of wood to the leasing of the big house ballroom (which Lord Headfort did in the late nineteenth century). Landlords also drew income from investments, demesne farming, and turbary (the sale of turf). Some landlords drew urban as well as agricultural rents. These accounts indicate the role of the estate in the wider community. They shed light on the benevolence of landlords, their interest in estate improvements, and the importance of the estate as a source of employment. Most particularly they give a good indication of the wealth or indebtedness of a landlord in the nineteenth century. In using such accounts, a working knowledge of double entry book-keeping is essential. Furthermore, expenditure accounts usually include remittances paid to the landlord and his dependents which should be considered when balancing income against the cost of maintaining the actual estate.

An estate collection may also include demesne farm account books recording farm profits and losses on an annual basis, as well as the stock on hand at the end of each accounting year. These account books help to increase our understanding of the significance of demesne farming to landlords in the nineteenth and twentieth centuries.[13]

Lease books are important for what they reveal about agricultural practices. A typical lease gave details of its duration, the names of the landlord and tenant, the amount of land leased, the annual rent or consideration charged, and any special clauses or covenants. In March 1842, for example, Henry Bruen of Oak Park, Co Carlow, entered into a lease with two of his tenants Thomas Booth senior and Thomas Booth junior, for a holding of eighty-seven acres at £1. 4s. 8d. per acre per year for the duration of the lives of those named in the lease. The lease described the location of the lands, and reserved all game, fishing, mines, minerals, coals, limestone, timber and turf rights to the landlord. It contained covenants regarding the payment of rent and the right to distrain for rent in the event of non-payment. It also contained covenants making the lessee responsible for planting ditches with white thorn quick sand building fences. It specified penalties for failing to do so. There were covenants for keeping land and premises in repair and free from trespass, forbidding the lessee from sub-letting or sub-dividing, cutting turf or building houses without the landlord's consent. A lease book or collection of leases can offer an insight into the nature of land tenure on an estate, the levels of rent, and often dates and reasons for evictions. From 1870 many leases show the lengths to which landlords were prepared to go in order to evade the payment of compensation under the terms of the 1870 Land Act.[14]

Estate maps and surveys are also valuable sources.[15] Prior to the Ordnance Survey of the 1830s (see below pp 59–60), cartography, surveying and landscape map production depended largely on the interest of landlords in these disciplines. In the late eighteenth and early nineteenth centuries many landlords, particularly larger ones, employed surveyors to provide an overview of their estates and cartographers to produce maps of their property as their prosperity increased.[16] Surveys provide a good deal of information on tenants, their holdings and the rents they paid. A survey of Lord Cloncurry's Kildare estate in 1838 is divided according to townland. The name of the occupier of each holding is specified and a description of the lot such as 'steep, rockey [sic], arable, very shallow, furzy'; 'fine soil for tillage. Medium quality rather coarse pasture' is recorded. The quantity of land held by occupiers is given in both Irish and English acres along with the rent per acre and the poor law valuation of the holding.[17]

In the early 1830s, James Edward Vaughan carried out a detailed survey of Lord Clonbrock's estate in Co Galway. He produced a general map to the scale of 3 inches to 1 mile. This map outlines the main features of the estate such as roads, waterways, bogs and woods. It marks out field divisions and there is an index which gives the names of the tenant who held each field. It offers information on the quality of the land demarcating arable and upland pasture, improved cut bog, inferior boggy pasture, improved mountain, bog and waste.[18]

The most valuable estate maps are those, such as Vaughan's, which outline and number each holding and are accompanied by a survey sheet which acts as an index to the tenants in possession of each numbered holding. There is a valuable collection of similar maps in the National Library which were drawn up by William Longfield in the late eighteenth and early nineteenth centuries. The index to this collection is available in the manuscript reading room. It is divided according to county. There are maps available for estates in all thirty-two counties although there are substantially more maps available for the Leinster counties (maps for Co Kildare alone account for twenty-seven pages of the index).[19]

The accuracy of estate maps may be questionable; however, such maps, in the absence of other source material, have added considerably to our understanding of pre-Famine economic and social development. They allow the researcher to study the physical characteristics of the landscape of an estate which in turn offers suggestions as to the social and economic circumstances of the landlord who owned it. They may provide information on the extent and nature of enclosures, changes in settlement patterns, the development of road networks, the nature of outoffices on an estate, or the nature of the demesne. Maps and accompanying surveys may also provide information on the duration of a tenant's occupancy, the rent he was paying, and may indicate if the landlord felt his income could be increased by raising the rent of this holding in the future.

For an insight into the management and day to day running of an estate, the agent's letter books are a very informative source. These contain copies of outgoing and incoming correspondence between agent and landlord, or agent and tenants on a daily basis. This material reveals important information on estate business including agricultural practice; the level of rents; difficulties caused by agitation or agricultural depression; employment practices; changing market conditions and the need to adopt different strategies in the management of the estate. A perusal of the vast collection of correspondence for the Ormonde estate for the early years of the 1880s reveals much about the agent's difficulties of collecting rents at that time. In 1883, he wrote to a small tenant: 'I must ask you to remit *at once* to this office the sum of £4.10s. being one and a half year's rent due by you to 1 May last. If I have not a satisfactory reply without delay I must place the matter in the hands of Lord Ormonde's solicitor'.[20] It is interesting to note the agent's change of tone when he wrote some time later to a much larger tenant who was over £98 in arrears: 'Lord Arthur Butler ... will feel much obliged by your kindly sending a remittance to this office for half years rent ... Lord Arthur would not trouble you so soon but is just now closing the accounts for year 1883'.[21] A study of this type of correspondence may be enlightening, not only regarding estate management, but also, for example, with respect to the different type of relationships which may have existed between a landlord and his large tenants and a landlord and his smaller tenants.

Estate correspondence is one of the few sources available which offer an insight into the world of the tenantry and a landlord's or his agent's policy towards them. For example, the Farnham estate correspondence in the National Library of Ireland for the late nineteenth century suggests that in the main, tenants seem to have written directly to Lord Farnham who, in turn, having read their letters, passed them on to his agent, T.R. Blackley, with any queries or suggestions he may have had. In September 1898 a tenant named Rose Cahill, wrote to Farnham:

> I beg to let your lordship know that I lost a good cow from a broken back last November crossing a ditch. Shortly after that I lost a yearling calf from blackleg. And another calf this year in February from redwater ... I have never entered courts and I hope you will consider my distress and allow me a little on account of the unavoidable death of my cattle.

Farnham passed the letter to Blackley who wrote a note back to him stating that: 'I had to take proceedings at the quarter sessions against Rose Cahill. I do not know whether her statement is true, but I would not recommend any gratuity'.[22] Blackley's comment is in itself a warning to the historian to be discerning when approaching such correspondence and to guard against the manipulative actions of certain shrewd Irish tenants so often caricatured by the likes of Somerville and Ross.

Ejectment books are unfortunately a rarer source. Amongst the most valuable of those in existence are two books of Earl Fitzwilliam's estate in Wicklow and Wexford for the years 1845 to 1886. These books record the notices to quit served annually and in many cases the reasons for their service. They reveal a good deal about the eviction process: tenants were not just ejected for non-payment of rents or accumulated arrears (although this was the most common reason); notices to quit were served for unauthorised sub-letting, bad husbandry (or farming practices), and for admitting lodgers.[23] Serving a notice to quit did not necessarily lead to actual eviction. In the Fitzwilliam ejectment books comments such as 'settled' or 'postponed' indicate that tenants and landlord came to some sort of arrangement regarding the payment of rents. Similarly, the fact that the same names appear time and time again in these books suggests that the notice to quit was used as a warning rather than as a sanction.

In a work of this length, it is not possible to discuss all of the various types of records which may be available in an estate collection. What has been described above are those sources which are most important for the study of estate management. But a comprehensive estate collection such as the Ormonde collection in the National Library, besides containing all of the sources referred to above, also contains items which may be of value to those interested in more specialised areas. For example, the collection contains a register of petitions to the agent from tenants for the years 1845–62 which offers a great deal of information on the effects of the Famine and its aftermath on the estate. For those interested in landlord improvements, the collection contains a list of houses built on the estate from 1854 to 1880. There is a register of tenants showing the amounts advanced to them in order to improve their holdings with details of the improvements carried out during the same years. There is also a register of rebates granted to tenants for improvements implemented during the years 1865–88.

Furthermore, the collection includes a register of tenants relating to judicial rent agreements granted in the Land Commission courts between 1884 and 1905; an account book of tenants who were constituted as caretakers from 1887 to 1897; and a set of tenants' notebooks for the years 1885–1923. There are copies of proposals for the sale of holdings to tenants (both judicial and non-judicial) on the estate in 1904, a year after the passing of the Wyndham Land Act, when most of the Ormonde estate was sold off. There are a number of important lists of people in the collection including a record of those invited to balls at Kilkenny Castle (which provides an insight to the narrow social circles in which the landed class moved); an alphabetical list of landowners in Kilkenny and the south-east compiled sometime between 1900 and 1916 and an alphabetical list of the tenants on the estate for the years 1880–85, essentially the period of the land war.

Estate records are undoubtedly the most valuable and important sources available to the historian attempting to reconstruct the development when applicable, and demise of an Irish estate. Rentals, accounts, surveys or valuations, letter books, maps and leases all help in the overall construction of an account of estate life. Information on rent movements may be gleaned from parliamentary papers or even newspapers but it is really only rentals which reveal the true picture.

Unfortunately, however, researching estate records is not without its share of problems. Firstly, only a small percentage of estate records have survived.

Larger estates and Ulster estates are better represented than small estates or those in the other three provinces of Leinster, Connnaught and Munster. Furthermore, much fewer estate records have survived for the pre-Famine period than for the post-Famine period. There are a number of reasons for this low survival rate. It is probable that a great deal of landlords, particularly those of lesser means, were not as likely to store estate records over generations as were larger landowners such as the Downshires, Ormondes or Clonbrocks. Indeed, proper accounts may not have been kept at all on some estates in the absence of a high degree of organisation and a dutiful agent. If a landlord served as his own agent, as many smaller landlords were obliged to do, he did not generate the same amount of records.

Frequently material held in the custody of family solicitors or land agency firms was disposed of.[24] Similarly, many estate collections were undoubtedly destroyed during the revolutionary period in Ireland when around 300 big houses were burned. From the 1920s onwards those who bought big houses, including the Land Commission, or indeed many of those who inherited them, saw little of value in cumbersome ledgers. Some were destroyed *in situ*; some found their way to local archives and local libraries; some were retained by interested relatives or friends while others were taken for curiosity value and subsequently hidden away in attics or out offices.[25]

Those papers now in private keeping are largely of a fragmentary nature. But all fragments are crucial in creating the history of an estate. As Donnelly concluded regarding his hunt for existing collections: 'After exhaustive searches in public and private archives in England and Ireland as well as attics, cellars, stables and barns throughout Co Cork, enough has been discovered to furnish a solid basis upon which to reconstruct the framework of estate administration and to measure its impact on the rural economy and the land question'.[26]

With respect to estate collections which remain in the possession of families, solicitors or land agency firms, it is not always possible to gain access to them. If they are accessible it may be at limited times and sometimes even at a cost to the researcher. The fragmentary nature of most collections, whether in private hands or repositories, brings related problems.[27] Ideally, for the study of the economics of a landed estate, for example, a series of estate ledgers and accounts should be available for the entire period under study. Furthermore, they should be legible and organised in a systematic manner so as to provide such information which lends itself to monitoring the changes in rents from year to year. Unfortunately, this ideal is too often unattainable – many series of estate rentals are broken or incomplete. As W.E. Vaughan has emphasised, when studying the economics of an estate, one has to be prepared to invest a considerable amount of time and effort in order to come to terms with the accounting system.[28]

III. TITHE APPLOTMENT BOOKS

Tithe applotment (or composition) books were compiled between 1823 and 1837 to assess the monetary tithes which were payable to the Church of Ireland under the Irish Tithe Composition Acts.[29] During this period holdings in each civil parish were valued based on the average price of wheat and oats in the parish during the seven years preceding 1 November 1821. Around 2,500 of these parish returns are available for consultation in the National Archives. These are the surviving originals for the twenty-six counties, although copies of those pertaining to the six counties are also available. The original books relating to the latter are available in P.R.O.N.I. The National Library has copies of the books on microfilm, while many county libraries and other local repositories have microform copies pertaining to local areas.

In order to consult the tithe applotment books, the researcher needs to know the names of the civil parishes in which an estate was located. Indexes available in the main repositories make it easy to locate the books pertaining to these parishes.[30] The townlands within the parish are listed alphabetically. No central authority supervised the conduct of the valuation, so the same information is not available for each parish. For most holdings one can find the name of the occupier, the area of his holding, a valuation and a record of the tithe payable. There are some books which merely state the amount of tithe payable for each holding. On the other hand, there are books for some parishes which give a great deal more information than was required. The latter often provide an insight into topics such as pre-Famine land divisions, rents per acre paid by tenants, whether the rundale system was prevalent in an area, and the type of crops grown by individual tenant farmers.

Tithe applotment books do not exist for every parish.[31] They contain no information about the landless who were exempt from the payment of tithes. Nor, as stated earlier, are they always particularly illuminating. Unfortunately, there are no accompanying maps to show land division on a field-by-field basis. Furthermore, the researcher will find difficulties in actually interpreting the quality of land described as 'marsh and arable'.

IV. GRIFFITH'S VALUATION

If a researcher is in any doubt about the identity of a landlord in a particular area during the mid-nineteenth century, he or she is advised to consult the government valuation. This valuation, commonly referred to as Griffith's valuation as it was carried out under the supervision of Sir Richard Griffith, is important not only in identifying landlords but as a source for the study of the landed estate in Ireland.[32] The valuation was carried out in the 1850s and

1860s and estimated the valuation of every holding in the country as a basis for local taxation. The printed valuation contains the names of every occupier of land or buildings in the country as well as the name of the immediate lessor (normally the landlord). Land and buildings were valued separarely. It is the first and only assessment of its type for the nineteenth century.

The source material of the valuation can be divided into three parts. Valuation manuscripts are the notebooks of the valuers who had been carefully trained by Griffith to value each holding. They consist of house books which record the names of occupiers and description of houses regarding their quality, length, breadth, height, number of measures, rate per measure and amount; tenure books detailing the contents of farms, rent, tenurial arrangements and general observations; and field books recording the amount of land, a description of the holding, quality of holding (taking into consideration such things as the quality of topsoil and subsoil, fertility, climate and proximity to markets) and value per statute acre. The books for the twenty-six counties of the present Irish Republic are available for consultation in the National Archives while those for the six counties of Northern Ireland are held in P.R.O.N.I.

The printed version of Griffith's valuation is based on the valuers' notebooks. A full collection can be found in the National Library.[33] If the names of the parishes and townlands comprising the estate are known, the researcher should consult the typed index to the primary valuation in the reading room in the National Library or the *Index to Griffith's valuation* published on microfilm by the All-Ireland Heritage Inc. in 1987. Counties are arranged alphabetically as are parishes within each county. A fiche reference for the parish is given, for example, 14.E.2 and refers only to the first exposure alluding to the particular parish. The list of householders for any one parish will usually run over a number of pages.

The valuation sheets are divided into a number of columns. Column 1 lists map references which are the key to the 6 inches to 1 mile ordnance survey maps. These references point the researcher towards the appropriate sheet of the six-inch map and to the number assigned by the valuators to each tenement within its townland. The Valuation Office kept copies of these maps and the same tenement numbers appear on them having been annotated in red ink.[34] By using both the printed valuation and the annotated maps together, one can create a comprehensive picture of what the tenurial geography of the mid-nineteenth century must have been like. Column 2 records the name of the townland and occupiers. Column 3 lists the name of the immediate lessor or landlord. Column 4, headed 'description of tenement', describes the tenant farmer's holding with reference to houses, offices and lands. A distinction is drawn between tenements which consisted of land only and tenements which had a house or other buildings located on it. Columns 5–8 detail the area of land held, the valuation of the land, the valuation of buildings and the total valuation of the holding.

So called cancelled books are especially important in tracing the changes in landownership in Ireland from the 1850s onwards. The Valuation Office kept a record of all changes in occupancy which took place from the completion of the valuation by keeping the manuscript copies of the original valuation and updating changes which took place by using different coloured inks. The cancelled books are organised in the same format as the printed valuation with the addition of an extra column at the end headed 'observations'. In this latter column, one may be occasionally lucky to find observations on the rent being paid for a holding, the existence and terms of a lease, the dimensions of a house or outoffices on the holding, or one may find a line drawn through the rateable valuation of a house with the observation that the house is 'down'. It is also worth examining the inside covers of each bound volume for additional information about a prominent landlord in the District Electoral Division to which the volume pertains. By examining the various coloured inks, one is able to trace the changes in lessor, occupier, area or valuation of holdings that have taken place over time. Where the name of the lessor changes following purchase under the various land acts, a stamp appears with the initials 'L.A.P.' signifying Land Purchase Act. These books are arranged by D.E.D., so when the researcher knows which townlands comprise an estate, he or she can check in the townlands index to find the relevant D.E.D. volumes which need to be consulted.

The books which pertain to the twenty-six counties of the Irish Republic are to be found in the Valuation Office and may be consulted on the payment of a prescribed fee (from which *bona fide* students are exempt). The books for the six counties of Northern Ireland are available in P.R.O.N.I. While photocopies of relevant pages are available, unless they are in colour they are useless as the keys to the changes in landownership are the different colours of ink used. It is, therefore, preferable to record relevant information while engaged in research at the repository. As this may be time consuming one should be as well prepared as possible before visiting the Valuation Office. It would therefore be beneficial to have to hand the name of the landlord that one is interested in along with the names of relevant townlands, parishes, baronies and D.E.D.s. It is advisable to bring four coloured pencils to record the changes of ownership as they appear in the books. The sheets of paper which one uses to record one's findings should be divided into columns as found in Griffith's valuation with an additional column included at the end and headed 'observations'.

Griffith's valuation has some limitations. Partnership farms held under the rundale system had their individual parcels bracketed together without being separately measured, thereby excluding certain tenant names.[35] One must also be careful in interpreting Griffith's rateable valuation as an indicator of the real letting value of land or as a measure of the rental income drawn by a landlord from his property. By the mid-1860s, with increased agricultural prosperity,

Griffith's valuation was around 15 per cent below the real letting value of land and by the 1870s at least 25–30 per cent below. Estate rentals are the only truly reliable source for tracing the letting value of estate lands in the decades following Griffith's valuation.

V. PARLIAMENTARY PAPERS

The term 'parliamentary paper' applies to bills, all papers printed by order of the House of Commons or House of Lords, and to papers presented to either or both houses by royal command.[36] For present purposes, the most relevant publications are reports of select committees and royal commissions, as well as the series of returns which parliament required of various departments in the course of its work. The fact that there are thousands of volumes of parliamentary papers makes it a most intimidating if not prohibitive source. But the researcher should not be put off by this; the initial problems associated with sorting through indexes will invariably lead to some detailed information either on place or subject.

Obviously in a work of this nature, it is only possible to discuss a very limited number of relevant papers. It will be necessary for the student researching the history of a landed estate to spend some time searching the various indexes in order to find other papers which may contain information pertaining to his or her area of study. Chapter 13 of volume four of Peter Cockton's *Subject catalogue of the House of Commons parliamentary papers, 1801–1900* (Cambridge, 1988) provides a listing of papers relevant to Ireland. The most relevant sub-section in this chapter is that which deals with agriculture and land. Full references are provided for each paper, including session, paper number, volume and page number and the filing number of the Chadwyck-Healey microfiche edition.[37] In order to consult the Chadwyck-Healey microfiche set one should refer to Peter Cockton's *House of Commons parliamentary papers, 1801–1900: guide to the Chadwyck-Healey microfiche edition* (Cambridge, 1991). The CD-ROM, Introduction to the index to the House of Commons parliamentary papers, is a cumulative index of all the House of Commons parliamentary papers published from 1801 to the 1990s, drawing together material from Chadwyck-Healey's *Subject catalogue of the House of Commons parliamentary papers, 1801– 1900*, the House of Commons decennial indexes covering the period 1900–79, and data from the Parliamentary Online Information Service database. In order to search for papers relevant to an area one can enter the name of the area under 'keyword' and if the name of the area appears in the title of one or more parliamentary papers, a listing will be given along with the reference to the parliamentary paper volume in which it can be located or the Chadwyck-Healey microfiche number. However, if the name of an area does not appear in the title of the paper, these indexes are of little value. Other recommended starting points are the bibliographies of secondary works relating to the Irish land question, some of which contain very comprehensive lists of parliamentary papers.[38]

Barbara Solow showed in the early 1970s how parliamentary papers could be used to offer a new and valuable insight into the land question.[39] Through her reliance on parliamentary papers she estimated the movement of rents, questioned many of the traditional views that saw landlords as capricious evictors, estimated the value of agricultural output and encouraged a new generation of historians to examine again the vicissitudes of landlords and tenants in nineteenth-century Ireland.

Solow drew much of her information from evidence presented to inquiries. A royal commission of inquiry was a group of persons appointed by the crown to inquire into the subject named by a royal warrant. It was composed of persons who were deemed to be experts in the subject to be investigated or who were experienced in public affairs. They held sittings in a variety of locations throughout the country and interviewed scores of witnesses from different backgrounds. Findings and conclusions were presented in report form along with the minutes of evidence taken by the commission. Select committees were comprised of members of the House of Commons or members of the House of Lords selected to conduct investigations into particular subjects.[40] The output of select committees are made up of the report on the subject investigated as well as a day-to-day record of the committees proceedings and minutes of evidence taken by the committee. The local historian can sometimes be fortunate to find an amount of material of local interest in the minutes of evidence.

In 1843, Sir Robert Peel the British Prime Minister agreed to appoint a royal commission to enquire into the occupation of land in Ireland. Officially entitled a *Report from her majesty's commissioners of inquiry into the state of law and practice in respect of the occupation of land in Ireland*, it took its abbreviated title, as was the norm, from its chairman, becoming better known as the Devon commission.[41] The commission received evidence from 1,100 witnesses including landlords, tenants, agents and land surveyors from all parts of Ireland. The end product was three massive volumes of evidence from which information can be culled on rent movements, valuation, the con-acre system, sub-letting, tenurial agreements, middlemen and absenteeism in pre-Famine Ireland. If one is interested in studying a particular estate in the years before the Famine, it is worth finding out if the landlord, agent, tenants, or all three gave evidence to this commission.

In 1881 the report and evidence of the Bessborough commission was presented to parliament.[42] It had been appointed to enquire ostensibly into the 1870 Land Act and amending acts but really was intended to deal with the crisis of the land war. It held sixty-five sittings from September 1880 to

January 1881 throughout the country and heard evidence from around eighty landlords, seventy agents, 500 tenants and a variety of land agents, land surveyors, valuers, agricultural experts, MPs, clergymen, solicitors, barristers and an assortment of other officials. Again, the evidence ranged over a wide diversity of landed-estate related topics, covering much of the post-Famine period from the 1850s to the early days of Land Leagueism and the land war. Similarly, in 1886, the Cowper commission was appointed to enquire into the 1881 and 1885 Land Acts.[43] Over 300 witnesses from all over Ireland, with similar backgrounds to those who had given evidence to the Bessborough commission, were examined. The evidence of this commission is particularly valuable for the light it sheds on contemporaries' perceptions of the changes wrought by the agricultural depression from the late 1870s, the growth of agrarian agitation, declining rent levels, and increasing landlord indebtedness.

There are many more valuable reports which shed light on Irish landed estates in the nineteenth and early twentieth centuries. Some deal with other land acts,[44] or with evictions in a particular area such as the notorious evictions at Kilrush in Co Clare between 1847 and 1850 when 2,700 families were cleared from their holdings,[45] while others detail the conditions of the poor in pre-Famine Ireland,[46] the state of agriculture,[47] and the problem of congestion in Ireland at the beginning of the twentieth century.[48]

One should approach the evidence of commissions and committees with a degree of scepticism.[49] It is certainly true that landlords and their agents were disproportionately represented at inquiries. It is also true that those questioned gave their evidence to make a point and it is hardly an exaggeration to claim that the point made usually had a stated or implied grievance behind it. W.E. Vaughan makes the following relevant point regarding the nature of questioning at inquiries: 'All suffered from the weakness of any inquiry that proceeded by asking direct questions: not only was there a risk of receiving misleading answers, but the questions themselves imposed a rigid simplicity on complicated matters.'[50] However, one should not lose sight of the fact that the minutes of evidence gathered by the various committees and commissions can be used to probe how contemporaries interpreted the so called 'land question' and analyse the fears and aspirations of landlords and tenants. Cross reference to other primary sources will help to reduce bias and provide a corrective to any information of a statistical nature.

A particularly useful parliamentary source for those studying the landed estate is the *Return of owners of land of an acre and upwards, in the several counties, counties of cities, and counties of towns in Ireland* [C1492], HC 1876, lxxx, 61. This lists alphabetically every owner of one acre of land and upwards in Ireland, giving their address, the size of their holding and the valuation of their land. Also of use in this respect is the *Return for 1870 of landed proprietors in each county, classed according to residence, showing extent and value of property held by each class – , and similar return of number of landed proprietors in each province* HC 1872,

20,663. Have you thought about the Land Purchase Bill ?—Yes; there is a landlord in my neighbourhood thinking about it, Mr. Leader.

20,664. Did he offer to sell to the tenants ?—Yes.

20,665. Do you know what he asked ?—He wants 20 years' purchase on the judicial rents, and his tenants offered him 17 years' purchase.

20,666. Are they likely to come to terms ?—I think so, some of them at least.

20,667. Do you think it would be an advantage to tenants to purchase. Would it. stimulate them to industry and to taking a greater interest in their land ? —It would undoubtedly. I think if the farmers got the land at a fair price the country would prosper and

you would not have any crime, for it is poverty that makes the people troublesome and brings crime into the country.

20,668. It is the low price of produce that has rendered you unable to meet your present engagements ? —Certainly. I did not get one penny of an abatement on my rent, not a copper.

20,669. Did you apply for an abatement ? — Oh, indeed, it was not for want of asking, and when times are depressed it ought to be the interest of the landlord to give an abatement.

20,670. Lord *Milltown.*—You hope to get back into your farm again ?—I do, sir.

Nov. 17 1886.

Martin Forrest.

The Commissioners adjourned their sittings until the 2nd December, at Dublin.

TWENTY-EIGHTH DAY.

Thursday, December 2nd, 1886.

The Commission met at 36, Merrion Square, Dublin, at 11 o'clock.

PRESENT :

THE RIGHT HON. EARL COWPER, President.

THE RIGHT HON. EARL OF MILLTOWN.
SIR JAMES CAIRD, K.C.B.

MR. NELIGAN, Q.C., Recorder of Londonderry.
MR. KNIPE.

LORD CLONCURRY examined.

20,671. The *President.*—I believe you farm yourself personally, Lord Cloncurry, a great deal ?—Yes, my lord, I farm a considerable quantity of land myself.

20,672. In which county or counties ?—In the home counties. I have in Kildare, Dublin, and Meath, in my own hands, 2,300 of my own land and 300 acres that I rent from the Court of Chancery. I also hold, in connexion with that, 1,300 acres of rough mountain land, for winterage, in the county Galway.

20,673. Would you be able to tell us what has been the state of agricultural interests lately—I suppose your experience is that there has been a large fall in the price of produce during the last few years ?—There has been a fall no doubt; that fall has not affected the men in the home counties, who, like myself, fatten cattle for the English and Scotch markets.

20,674. Sir *James Caird.*—Are the 2,300 acres in your own hand all in grass ?—Yes, practically. There is no tillage or plantations or waste of any kind included in the figures I am giving to you. I speak only as to cattle—from personal experience. I have been keeping for the last 10 or 12 years a record of the weight of my cattle, both at the time of buying and selling, and an accurate account of the buying and selling prices, and I can give you such information as these entries afford. They show this, however, that the fall has come upon the men in the western districts who sell store cattle, and that men in the eastern counties, such as myself, have not experienced any fall. The actual profits of this year were within a few shillings the same as the average of the last 10 years, and considerably better than the average of the last two years. Taking, for instance, the years 1876 and 1886, the buying in price of my store cattle —the average on about 1,000 head of bullocks—in 1876 was £14 12s., and the selling price £21 6s.; while this year the buying in price was £8 9s., and the selling price has been £16 10s. Of course, all the figures I have show that the price of store cattle, which I buy in September, October, and November in one year for the purpose of selling off the grass in

the following year, has been steadily going down in the counties where I buy—chiefly in Mayo and Galway, and that the selling price (I sell all in Glasgow, Northampton, Wakefield, and Islington) has gone down too, but not more than the price of the stores. The result is that I am about in *statu quo*, for the last ten years, and rather better this year than usual.

Dec. 2, 1886.

Lord Cloncurry.

20,675. The *President.*—And really all your farming depends upon that ?—Yes.

20,676. Buying stores, fattening them, and selling in the English markets ?—Yes.

20,677. And in that particular department of agriculture there has been no loss of late years ?—There has been no loss to those who bought stores, as I did, and prepared them for the butcher. All my cattle are sold off the land in a very fair condition for the butcher.

20,678. And would it be the same with sheep ?— I would not like to say for certain as to that. My land does not suit sheep very well, and I confine my operations practically to cattle.

20,679. The result of your figures is that your profits have averaged much about the same for the past 10 years ?—Yes, and this year I am about £3 a head better than in 1884 and 1885. The year 1882 was a most extraordinary year, and that upsets the average somewhat—the prices were beyond reason in that year ; I made £13 a head on every beast I sold in 1882. Of course I am speaking of gross profits, my lord ; I don't mean these figures as net.

20,680. Is there anything else with regard to your farming experiences that you think it would be useful for us to know?—Do you mean on the general question——

20,681. On the question of your own farming. I think, seeing that your experience is confined to the one department, we have pretty well exhausted what you can have to say on that topic ?—Yes; but with your permission, I would like to express an opinion upon another subject. As I have already mentioned, I don't only farm my own lands, but I am a tenant of 300 acres under the Court of Chancery, on lease ; and

4. Extract from *Report of the royal commission on the Land Law (Ireland) Act, 1881, and the Purchase of Land (Ireland) Act, 1885; minutes of evidence and appendices.* [C4969–I], HC 1887, xxvi, 25. [Earl Cowper, chairman].

(167), xlvii. A return for 1906 gives a good indication of the size of demesnes in Ireland and the amount of untenanted land in the possession of landlords in rural districts at that time. The poor law valuation of this land is also recorded; thus one can determine whether the untenanted land held by a landlord was held for grazing or farming purposes or whether it was of little economic benefit by virtue of its being mainly wasteland.[51] There are also a number of important returns relating to, for example, the sales of estates under the Encumbered Estates Act[52]; the Arrears of Rent Act[53]; the estates purchased by the Congested Districts Board[54]; and the average number of years purchase on rents received for estates under the various land purchase acts from 1870 to 1903.[55]

With regard to the Irish landed estate, perhaps the most important returns are those which were termed 'returns of advances'. Effectively these were returns of the advances made to tenants by the Irish Land Commission under the land acts from 1881 to enable them to purchase their holdings.[56] Unfortunately, under the earlier land acts (1881, 1885 and 1891), there are no general indexes of estates sold which would otherwise save the researcher much searching. In the early returns, estates sold are listed according to counties. Obviously, if a landlord had property in a number of counties, sales in all these counties should be consulted. General indexes to estates sold under the 1903 and 1909 Land Acts are available.[57] For the sale of estates after 1921, the researcher should consult the *Iris Oifigiúil* which is available in the National Library. This source deals in particular with estates sold under the Free State Land Acts from 1923 onwards. It does not offer the same detail as the return of advances but one can still estimate the amount of land sold by a landowner, its location and how much he was paid.

The value of the returns of advances can be best illustrated in the following manner. Using the *Return of advances made under the Irish Land Purchase Acts during the months of July, August and October 1919* HC 1921 [cmd 1298], xviii, one pursues the following steps: firstly, there is an index listing alphabetically the names of the landowners whose estates feature in this paper. If the researcher's subject is listed here he or she need simply go to the relevant page(s). The index is followed by a 'summary of advances made during the months ... by the Estates Commissioners'. This summary is comprised of twelve columns detailing the date on which the advance was made; the name of the estate; the Land Commission record number; the name of the county; the number of purchasers on that estate; the area purchased; the current rent of the holdings sold; the price paid; the amount of advance; the amount of payment in cash; the number of years purchase of rent; and column 12 was reserved for observations.[58] In cases where more specific details are required one proceeds to the relevant pages as specified in the index. Here details are given regarding the name of the purchasers, the acreage they bought and its townland location, along with a record of its tenement valuation, its rent and details of whether the rent was judicial or non-judicial (that is whether it had been fixed or not under the fair rent fixing terms of the 1881 Land Act). The price paid for the holding is specified as is the amount of the advance and, or the amount paid in cash by the purchaser and the number of years purchase on current rents which the purchase price represented.

With this type of information available so much is possible for the researcher, especially if used in conjunction with estate records. One can obviously trace the sale of an estate under the various land acts. It is interesting to see when landlords sold their properties. Did some smaller sales of outlying properties by large landowners, for example, take place under the 1881 and 1885 Land Acts and was this perhaps determined by the agricultural crisis and agitation which characterised the early 1880s? Did landlords who were reluctant to sell under the early land acts rush onto the market when the Wyndham Act of 1903 offered them a 12 per cent bonus for the sale of estates? Did a landlord who did not sell in the years directly following 1903 do so after it became obvious in 1908 that the terms under the act which was to follow in 1909 would not be as generous? How much of his estate did a landlord retain in demesne and untenanted land in order that he might continue as a substantial farmer? How much of an estate was compulsorily acquired under the Free State Land Acts? If information on estate charges is available in estate records, it may be possible to estimate how much capital was left to a landlord from sales after charges were redeemed.

Another set of returns which are important are those dealing with the judicial rents fixed by the Irish Land Commission under the terms of the 1881 Land Act. Again, these returns can be located by reference to the indexes named above. They were compiled on a monthly basis and offer the following information: firstly, each paper begins with a useful index to the counties in which cases were determined. There is then a summary, showing according to counties and provinces, the number of cases in which judicial rents were fixed during the month; the acreage; tenement valuation; former rents and new judicial rents. For each county, the information is divided into ten columns recording the names of the sub-commissioners who heard the case; the Irish Land Commission number of the case; the name of the tenant; the name of the landlord; the name of the townland; the size of the holding in statute acres; the tenement valuation; the former rent of the holding; the judicial rent and observations (which include, for example, the dates of when previous rent changes had taken place).

The information in these returns can be supplemented by reports of various government bodies published as parliamentary papers such as the annual reports of the Congested District Board from 1892 to 1921 and the annual reports of the Irish Land Commission and the Estates Commissioners. British Parliament also published a range of accounts and statistics annually. The material in these was usually presented on a local basis rendering it a valuable source for local historians. From 1847, for example, the annual returns of agricultural produce in Ireland were presented on a county by county basis. Counties were then broken down into poor law unions and further divided into electoral districts. These statistics provide information on crops and livestock, the number and size of farms and the output from a range of different farm sizes, thereby facilitating the construction of a picture of a local economy from one year to the next.

As stated earlier, parliamentary papers present an imposing volume of possible research material. A considerable amount of time will need to be spent searching through relevant indexes to source the papers that will be of most value to the local historian. However, the tedium of such searching will invariably be rewarded by the information found in the end. The National Library houses most of them and indexes can be consulted at the desk or on CD-ROM in the reading room. The Chadwyck-Healey microfiche set has helped make parliamentary papers more accessible. To consult an original paper in the National Library one needs to know the date of the parliamentary session and the volume number. For example, the title and reference number of one parliamentary paper footnoted below reads as follows: *Return of estates purchased by the Congested Districts Board for Ireland in respect of the period of six months ended 30 April 1904, for the purpose of resale to tenants and the enlargement of holdings*, HC 1904, lxxx, 525. 1904 is the session number; lxxx is the bound volume number; and 525 is the page number.

VI. THE RECORDS OF THE IRISH LAND COMMISSION
AND CONGESTED DISTRICTS BOARD

The Land Commission was set up in 1881 under the land act of that year. It became primarily responsible for the advancement of monies to tenants to enable them to purchase their holdings and the fixing of fair rents under the various land acts from 1881 onwards. As the commission had to be satisfied that potential purchasers would be able to repay their annuities it employed inspectors to assess the capacity of tenants to make their repayments. Therefore, the Land Commission records are one of the few sources which reveal as much about tenants as about landlords.[59] The records in the Land Commission Records Branch office can be divided into three main areas – those dealing with land purchase; those dealing with the fixing of fair rents; and those belonging to the Congested Districts Board.[60]

Land purchase records are arranged according to estates. Edward Keane has catalogued the documents available for individual estates in the Land Commission and this catalogue is available for consultation in the National Library.[61] This is an important starting point for anybody wishing to consult the Land Commission records. The card index file in the reading room is arranged by estate name and county. Each card contains a number (or numbers) which refer to the series of green volumes, also in the reading room, in which there are summaries of what is contained in the box of records for an estate in the Land Commission offices. For example, looking up the Clonbrock estate in the card index, one firstly finds the name of the sitting landlord at the time of the sale of the estate and the names of the baronies in which the estate was located. The number 'E.C. 7159' refers to the green volumes and 'box no. 3436' to the Land Commission reference. In the green volume one finds that 'box 3436' should contain such records as deeds for 1803 to 1907; a rental for 1909; the Land Commission inspector's report; records relating to conveyances in the nineteenth century; maps of the estate; and copies of the original wills of former owners of the estate.

Most estate files in the Land Commission office contain all the records of the various stages leading to the completion of the sale of an estate during the late nineteenth and early twentieth centuries. However, there are no originating statements or final schedule on incumbrances for sales under the 1881 Land Act in existence. Unfortunately, neither has any of the actual Land Commission correspondence survived, seemingly having been destroyed around 1946.[62] From the records which have survived one can trace the economic history of an estate from the mid-1880s onwards. Landlords had to prove title to their estates and the Land Commission had to be assured of its authenticity, so abstracts of titles and title deeds are contained in each file. An originating application records the name of the vendor, and the location and nature of tenure of the property. An abstract of title gives details of the title and details how the estate came to be in the hands of the landlord, while deeds and wills presented by the landlord to the Land Commission prove the statements in the abstract.

The commission had to be secure in the knowledge that tenants would be able to afford to repay their annuities on their advances which necessitated inspectors making detailed studies of even the smallest holdings. Inspectors' reports are, therefore, of great value in determining the quality of holdings, tenurial arrangements, rental capacity and tenants' ability to pay their rents. As the introduction to Edward Keane's catalogues point out, this, therefore, is one of the few sources which is informative regarding the socio-economic life of the tenantry. Herein one finds details on the type of agriculture practiced on a holding – whether grazing, tillage or mixed – the conditions of the farm; what improvements had been carried out and whether implemented by land-lord, tenant or both; the customary rights tenants had to mountain grazing or turbary; the proximity to local markets; and the quality of house and out-offices occupied and used by tenants.

Accompanying surveyors' reports outlined any problems associated with subletting, joint tenancies or fragmentation and indicated how these might be solved. K.L. Buckley makes the interesting point that:

evidence as to sub-tenants is particularly important, and their existence was a constant source of trouble to tenants attempting to obtain an advance from the Land Commission to purchase their holdings: it is noteworthy how quickly their sub-tenants, when noted on an inspector's report on a holding, tend to become transformed into grazing tenants, holding under caretaker or conacre agreements – and, therefore, no longer technically tenants – once the would be purchasing tenants realised that their presence as sub-tenants was a barrier to his plans.[63]

A schedule of tenancies for each estate records the names of occupying tenants at the time of purchase which is illuminated by an accompanying reference map on the scale of 6 inches to 1 mile.[64]

An important source is the final schedule of incumbrance pertaining to each estate, some of which can run up to thirty pages in length. These detail the charges on an estate at the time of sale, recording mortgages, family charges, jointures, and superior interest such as quit rent, head rent and tithe-rent charges. From these, as L.P. Curtis has shown, one can begin to assess the indebtedness of a landlord and estimate the capital left to him from sales after these charges had been met.

For the researcher interested in the fixing of fair rents, the Land Commission records contain files on nearly half a million cases. These show the level of reductions granted either by the Land Commission, the Civil Bill Court, or upon agreement between landlord and tenant in the case of first, second and third term rents.[65] There are, fortunately, registers available which are indexed with the names of landlords and usually tenants. For all cases after 1896, when second term rents were fixed, there are valuers' reports on holdings which contain much the same information as the aforementioned inspectors' reports.[66]

While the Land Commission records are amongst the most important archival collections available for any study of a landed estate in Ireland from the late nineteenth century onwards, they are, unfortunately, not readily accessible. In fact, with the exception of records such as schedules of tenancies, it is at present virtually impossible to gain access to records such as inspectors' reports for any estate. The argument put forward is that some of these are records of a sensitive and confidential nature. In view of the fact that many other historical documents of a similar 'sensitive' nature are freely available, this seems rather strange to say the least. Furthermore, several of the documents deposited in the Land Commission records are already available in some estate collections. The more likely explanation for the inaccessibility of these records is the lack of resources and manpower being made available to the Records Branch, in which case something needs to be done in order to promote scholarly research so as to enhance our understanding of the final days of landlordism in Ireland.

The Congested Districts Board was established under the 1891 Land Act to relieve the problem of congestion along the western seaboard. The 1896 Land Act empowered the board to secure advances from the Land Commission for the purchase of estates from landlords instead of having to buy them out of board funds. The 1903 and 1909 Land Acts further extended the powers of the board, making more money available and conferring authority upon it to compulsorily acquire land for the relief of congestion. By the time the board was dissolved in 1923 it had purchased 874 estates comprising 1.77 million acres. Under the terms of the 1923 Land Act, the records of the board were transferred to the Land Commission.

The inaccessibility of much of the board's records in the Land Commission offices can be somewhat offset by the availability of the baseline reports of the board's local inspectors which are available on microfilm in the National Library. Again these offer a good deal of information on landlords and tenants, particularly along the western seaboard where, in some areas, even by the late nineteenth century, rundale was still practiced. They sometimes offer information on the size of estates, the number and quality of holdings thereon, and their rental. They present a picture of the socio-economic environment of a locality by describing markets, fairs, postal and telegraph facilities. They describe in detail how farmers cultivated their lands and how they disposed of their farm produce. Effectively they provide an insight into the hardship of a tenantry who were operating at subsistence level on most western estates. There is also documentary evidence of the board's policy of promoting migration from these congested areas, a policy which was continued by the Land Commission from the 1920s when it settled migrants from congested areas in counties such as Meath and Kildare.[67]

Furthermore, one should be aware that much valuable information, statistical and otherwise, can be gleaned from the annual *Reports of the Congested Districts Board*, a listing of which can be found in the indexes to parliamentary papers.[68] Also of great importance are the dozen or so reports of the royal commission appointed to enquire into congestion in Ireland at the beginning of the twentieth century. Again reference to these can be found in indexes to parliamentary papers.[69]

VII. REGISTRY OF DEEDS

The Registry of Deeds was set up by the Registry of Deeds Act of 1707 'to secure purchasers and prevent forgeries and fraudulent gifts and conveyances of land, tenements and hereditaments,[70] which have been frequently practised in this kingdom, especially by Papists to the great prejudice of the Protestant interest thereof '. A central office was established in Dublin in which all transactions concerning land such as leases and mortgages were to be registered. Historians have largely shied away from using the voluminous information available in the Registry of Deeds.[71] There are over 4,000,000 memorials stored there dealing with property in Ireland from 1708. A memorial is a summary of a deed, recording the date of it, the names of the parties and witnesses to the deed, and a description of the property and its location. Memorials are more often than not sufficiently detailed to substitute for the original documents which may no longer be in existence.[72]

Dowries were a prime consideration in any marriage involving a member of a landlord's family, but particularly an eldest son who had the responsibility of passing on the family estate, big house and heirlooms to the next generation. Estates were kept intact by primogeniture. Therefore, a strict settlement was drawn up on the eldest son's marriage or on his reaching his majority entailing the estate on the eldest grandson (usually not yet born), which made the heir merely tenant for life. When an heir to an estate got engaged to marry, negotiations were entered into by both families over the settlement (which was business-based and as such took the form of a business arrangement). It was usually settled that a bride receive an annual allowance, known as 'pin money', while her husband was alive, and brought with her a dowry, which was often used to alleviate a financial burden of the family into which she married, or else provided the basis for her jointure. When, for example, Charles William Fitzgerald, marquis of Kildare, and heir to the duke of Leinster, married Lady Caroline, daughter of the duke of Sutherland, in 1847, the marriage settlement drawn up between both families first of all specified the rental of the Leinster estate which stood at around £24,000 per annum. The incumbrances on the estate were then outlined with a stipulation that 'Lady Caroline's fortune should be paid to the duke whose intention is to discharge with it incumbrances affecting his estate'. There was reference to sums to be invested, although not specified, which would 'secure to the marquis of Kildare during the joint lives of himself and the duke, £4,000 per annum, payable quarterly'. Provision was made for £600 per annum to be paid to Lady Caroline 'during the joint lives of herself and the marquis by way of pin money'; £2,500 to her during the joint lives of herself and the duke if the marquis died in the lifetime of the duke, and £4,000 per annum by way of a jointure if Lady Caroline was to survive the marquis and the duke.

The example above gives an indication of the type of information one can accumulate regarding an estate from the material stored in the Registry of Deeds: one may be able to ascertain the rental income of an estate; estimate the level of indebtedness of a landlord; investigate how marriage arrangements were used to alleviate some burdens; explore how the same arrangements could, in fact, add to the burden especially if a widow was to survive a husband by a number of years; and even discover how a marriage settlement allowed wives of landlords much greater liberty and equality than wives in the classes below them because of the pin money and jointures[73] guaranteed to them.

During the eighteenth and nineteenth centuries few landlords could raise the capital necessary for the payment of jointures without recourse to borrowing on mortgage. Therefore, mortgages, which record the amount of principal, the interest rate and the length of a loan, can tell much of a landlord's financial position at a given time. Indentures of conveyance cite prices of land sold and the terms of sale.[74] Leases, as discussed earlier, specify the position and quality of the property involved and give an insight into tenurial arrangements, rents and terms of their payment.

Notice is provided of the registration of a deed through the memorials and indexes which are available for inspection in the Registry of Deeds on payment of a prescribed fee. Some memorials contain incidental information such as references to previous deeds. Up to 1832, all memorials (almost 600,000 of them) were numbered consecutively. From 1833, memorials were filed in books of 300. To reference an individual memorial one needs to know the year in which it was registered, the book number and the memorial number within the book.

Researchers are advised to begin their search by consulting the transcript books into which memorials were copied up to 1960 and which are available for the years 1708–1960 (excluding 1951–6). The information in these books is more accessible and legible than in the original memorials. They are numbered in the same way as the memorials. They should be used in tandem with the names index books which is an index of all grantors since 1708. Prior to 1833, the names index contained the names of all grantors (but only the surname of the first grantee), a reference to the book in which the transcript is contained, the page number in the book and the memorial number. There is unfortunately no county reference. From 1833 onwards the names index also gives the first name of the first grantee, the county in which the land is situated and the full reference to the memorial (which is the same for the transcript). There are also three special names index books which deal solely with memorials filed by the Encumbered Estates Court for the years 1850–58. The difficulty for researchers interested in the pre-1833 period is that one is provided with very little information and so one must continuously refer to the transcripts which can be time consuming. Because the name of county is given for the post-1833 era, the amount of cross-checking is greatly reduced.

There are also land index books for 1708–1946 which are available for inspection. For 1708 to 1832, the index of lands is arranged by reference to county, townland and corporate town. A large number of years are covered in single books; for example, the first book in the series deals with the period 1708–38. The indexing is not altogether satisfactory. The arrangement of townlands in alphabetical order extends to the first letter only. One must also be wary of local variations in townland names and spellings. There was no obligation to use standardised townland names. Additional references were often put at the end of books. From 1833 the lands index is arranged by the county, barony and townland (again in alphabetical order, although not strictly so) and corporate towns. These books are kept in five year volumes and give details of the first grantor, first grantee, barony, townland, and registry reference of the memorial and transcript. Some entries are cramped into small spaces and may be difficult to read; a magnifying glass might be a useful tool for the researcher in this case. Copies of both the names index and the lands index are available on microfilm in the National Library of Ireland. Once the relevant entry in either index has been located, the researcher will then find a corresponding number which will match the transcript book to be consulted in the Registry of Deeds.

Upon a first visit to the Registry of Deeds one must be prepared to allow oneself plenty of time due to the very nature of the research. One must also consider the fact that the act establishing the Registry of Deeds had its origin in the penal laws. From 1704 no catholic could purchase a lease for more than thirty-one years nor could a catholic invest in mortgages. This remained the case until the 1780s and while this volume is essentially a guide to sources for the nineteenth and twentieth centuries it is worth noting that even if the penal laws were only intermittently stringently applied they nonetheless greatly reduced the number of transactions concerning catholics available in the Registry of Deeds. Also large landowners in general were lethargic about officially registering leases with their tenants, particularly those on small holdings. The socio-economic relationship between the two groups put very little onus on the landlord to do so and those leases which are registered are predominantly between more equal parties such as a small landowner and a prosperous tenant or a landlord and a head landlord. If one is interested in landlord policy regarding the granting of leases, and such information is not available from estate records, one would be advised to consult the tenure books of Griffith's valuation to ascertain whether tenants were described as 'tenants at will' in which case there is no lease and therefore no need to visit the Registry of Deeds.

VIII. ENCUMBERED ESTATES

As we have seen in the previous section, the (second) Encumbered Estates Act of 1849 was intended to facilitate the sale of insolvent estates. It led to the establishment of the Encumbered Estates Court. This court had the power to sell an estate without a landowner's consent if the estate was in receivership or if the level of debt on the estate was greater than half of the annual rental income. As a result of government legislation passed in 1858 and 1859, this court was replaced by a new body, the Landed Estates Court, which was wound-up in 1879.[75] There are five sequences of rentals which have survived pertaining to these courts – two of which are to be found in the National Library, two in the National Archives, and one in P.R.O.N.I.[76] The most complete sequence is that referred to as the O'Brien rentals stored in the National Archives and consisting of almost 150 volumes.[77] There is a considerable amount of overlapping in the five sequences, but there are indexes available in the various repositories which guide researchers to the landed estate under study if it was sold through the Encumbered Estates or Landed Estates Court.

The term 'rental' is something of a misnomer as these volumes contain a much greater wealth of information than simply the rental of an estate. The information pertaining to each estate usually includes, for example, an advertisement of sale of an estate, naming the owner and petitioner, stating where the sale was to take place, the date, and the number of lots in which the estate was to be sold. There are accompanying coloured maps of the property to be sold, each lot distinguished by a different colour. A map may also distinguish a landlord's residence and demesne (Some rentals contain illustrations of the big house on the property). Down to 1862, these maps were usually the work of valuators, but after that date they were official ordnance survey maps. The rentals of individual properties offered for sale are not uniform in content but are all divided into a series of columns which contain information such as the size of individual holdings in statute acres; the name of the townland in which it was located; the name of the occupier; Griffith's valuation; the poor law valuation; rents paid by tenants; gale days; tenurial arrangements of individual tenants; dates and lengths of leases where applicable and probable rent charges. This data is then followed by descriptive particulars of the individual lots such as: 'The principal part of the lands of this lot is good tillage soil; there is a large extent of bog attached'.

These rentals and accompanying documents are extremely valuable in recreating a picture of estate life in the mid-nineteenth century. Besides recording information on an estate's location and its hinterland, they offer data on the size and rental of individual holdings and tenurial arrangements, indicating whether tenants held 'at will' or by lease. They help to illustrate the extent of landlord indebtedness as a result of the Famine or indeed the effects which large-scale mortgaging to facilitate the building of big houses or the maintenance of a grand lifestyle had on estates.[78] Rentals show the state of neglect by some landlords before the Famine as a result of mismanagement or the detrimental effects of long leases for ninety-nine years granted in the eighteenth century; others show that several landlords became insolvent as a result of their efforts to relieve their tenants' destitution during the Famine. The rentals also testify that some landlords, such as George Moore of Moore Hall in Mayo, had to sell parts of their estates to remain solvent. Unfortunately, the rentals tell us nothing of the new proprietors. This is an aspect of the history of landed estates which has yet to be adequately examined. The use of these rentals in conjunction with the cancelled books in the Valuation Office might be one way of beginning to tackle it.

5. Encumbered Estates Rental, 1854: advertisement for sale of Ballintober
and Ballybanaun estates, property of George Henry Moore,
M.P. (courtesy of the National Library of Ireland).

IX. MEMOIRS, DIARIES, TRAVELLERS' GUIDES AND CONTEMPORARY WORKS

Although published memoirs, diaries, and contemporary works have their
limitations which will be discussed presently, such personal accounts should
not be dismissed as hopelessly biased or inaccurate.[79] Unfortunately, there are
all too few autobiographies and published memoirs of Irish landlords and
those that survive are often fragmentary and digressive. They tend to reveal
more about the social life of the landed class than the economics of landlordism or the management policy on estates.[80]

Some works were written during the turbulent years of the land war when
a number of landlords or their agents attempted to correct the imbalance of
the large number of books and pamphlets which attacked them and
landlordism. The autobiography of Sir William Gregory of Coole Park,
Co Galway, reveals his apprehensions and fears during the Land League days
of the early 1880s.[81] One needs to be discerning and critical in handling the
information contained in this work or in others such as William Bence-Jones's

The life's work in Ireland of a landlord who tried to do his duty (London, 1880) or William Steuart Trench's earlier *Realities of Irish life* (London, 1868). A number of other land agents have left their memoirs or collections of letters. William Robert Anketell's *Landlord and tenant: Ireland. Letters by a land agent* . . . (Belfast, 1869) records his comments on such subjects as leases, tenant improvements, tenant rights, capricious evictions, valuations and rents. S.M Hussey, one of the partners of Hussey and Townsend, probably the largest land agency firm in Ireland in the nineteenth century, has left his *The reminiscences of an Irish land agent* (London, 1904). For an agent's opinions on estate management in pre-Famine Ireland, see William Blacker, *Prize essay, address to the agricultural committee of the Royal Dublin Society, on the management of landed property in Ireland; the consolidation of small farms, employment of the poor etc. for which the gold medal was awarded* (Dublin, 1834). Also informative is 'One late an agent' (pseud.), *Landlordism in Ireland with its difficulties* (London, 1853); G.F. Trench, *Are the landlords worth preserving? or, forty years management of an Irish estate* (London and Dublin, 1881). For opinions of landlords on the land question in pre-Famine and post-Famine periods the Earl of Rosse's, *Letters on the state of Ireland by a landed proprietor* (London, 1847); the Knight of Kerry's *Irish landlords and tenants: recent letters to 'The Times' and further correspondence on the above subject* (Dublin, 1876); and John Hamilton, *Sixty years experience as an Irish landlord: Memoirs of John Hamilton, D.L., of St Ernan's, Donegal* (London, 1894) are worthy of study. D. Thomson and M. Mc Gusty (ed.), *The Irish Journals of Elizabeth Smith 1840–50* (Oxford, 1980) is most revealing regarding the Famine in County Wicklow.

Memoirs, published diaries and collections of letters such as these provide valuable impressions of how the members of the landed class or those associated with it interpreted events such as the Great Famine, the land war, or the rise of the Land League as they unfolded.[82] However, the weaknesses of such works must be kept in mind. They are, after all, collections of memories which are inevitably coloured by emotions and personal opinions. Memoirs are never all inclusive: because they are written retrospectively, they are selective. These memories are inevitably affected by nostalgia or resentment. The time lag between the experience and the recording of it may in some cases be a lengthy one which means the writer's recollection of events may be vague or inaccurate. There is the danger that a landlord or agent may have falsified information in order to present himself in a more favourable light to his audience. Published collections of letters and diaries are more immediate than memoirs and are therefore probably more reliable as evidence but even they need to be approached with a certain amount of scepticism: were letters written with a particular agenda in mind? Was the writer careful in expressing personal anxieties? Are entries edited so as to please the readership (or, indeed, even the writer)? One must establish the context in which the memoir was created by continuous reference to contemporary sources in order to check the validity of the writer's memories.

The nineteenth century also saw the publication of a great number of English and Continental travellers' accounts. These offer contemporary descriptions of places and people at particular times and some statistical information. They tend to be written by members of the upper or middle classes whose observations were dictated by ideological convictions, their own bias and prejudice, the agendas of the social class to which they belonged, or, indeed, as in the case of journalists such as Finlay Dun, the agenda of their employers.

Dun came to Ireland in the early 1880s and wrote a series of newspaper articles on Irish landlords and landed estates for *The Times* which were later published in book form as *Landlords and tenants in Ireland* (London, 1881). Despite its weaknesses, the book is an important source as it offers a valuable, if brief, insight into the management of twelve individual estates in Ireland at the beginning of the land war as well as more general information on estates in counties Cork, Kerry, Down, Antrim, Derry, Tyrone, Donegal and Mayo. In some cases, Dun gained access to family estate papers and reproduced information from them.[83]

George Pellew's *In castles and cabins or talks in Ireland* (London, 1888) and George Shaw Lefevre's *Incident of coercion. A journal of visits to Ireland 1882 and 1888* (London, 1889) offer accounts of landlord-tenant relations during the land war. Madame De Bovet's *Three month's tour in Ireland*, translated by Mrs Arthur Walter (London, 1891) contains a description of a monster meeting of the Irish National League in Waterford. For the Famine years see Marquis of Dufferin and Ava and G.F. Boyle, *Narrative of a journey from Oxford to Skibbereen during the years of the Irish famine* (Oxford, 1847) and [John Locke], *Ireland: Observations on the people, the land and the law in 1851; with especial reference to the policy, practice and results of the Encumbered Estates Court* (Dublin and London, 1852). For the pre-Famine period, H.D. Inglis's *A journey through Ireland during the spring, summer and autumn of 1834* (2 vols, London, 1834) offers an assessment of the effects of absentee landlordism in Ireland. Although Arthur Young's *A tour in Ireland, 1776–9* (A.W. Hutton ed., London, 1892) deals with the late eighteenth century it is worthy of consultation.[84]

While travellers' accounts may offer much valuable information, the researcher should be as discerning and critical with this information as with memoirs, diaries and autobiographies.[85] It is important to consider if the people being observed by the traveller allowed him or her to see only what they wanted the latter to see. Similarly one must question the reliability of the information with which landlords supplied the visitor. Dun estimated that the duke of Leinster expended 20 per cent of his annual rental income on estate improvements between 1875 and 1881,[86] whereas estate accounts show that the figure was in fact nearer to 14 per cent. Hence cross referencing is necessary, where possible, to constantly authenticate information, particularly statistical data.

X. NEWSPAPERS

In his *Land and people of nineteenth-century Cork,* J.S. Donnelly jr. has shown the benefits to the local historian of making extensive use of newspapers as a source of information. Through a comprehensive study of local newspapers such as the *Cork Advertiser, Cork Constitution* and the *Cork Examiner,* Donnelly gathered valuable information on landed estates in County Cork and investigated the manner in which they were affected by the Famine, agricultural depression, and the land war. Yet, although newspapers are one of the most accessible sources, they have remained largely unexploited.[87]

By the late nineteenth century most counties in Ireland had at least one newspaper. Local newspapers can indicate what landlord-tenant relations were like in an area. They provide information on the social and economic conditions of tenants which is not often available in estate papers. They can very often provide graphic accounts of evictions and while landlords' reasons for evictions may be available in estate papers, newspapers are one of the few sources available that may offer some insight into tenants' reactions to these evictions. Local newspapers contain accounts of rent strikes; they record levels of abatements granted by individual landlords; they may provide reports of landlord attempts at Famine relief in the late 1840s; or report cases heard by the Land Commission courts from the early 1880s. They sometimes contain copies of memorials from tenants to landlords or communications received by tenants from their landlords, the originals of which may no longer exist. Newspapers also publish reports on local fairs and markets with useful details of cattle and agricultural prices down through the years. They may also feature advertisements of sales pertaining to estates or big houses and their contents. Weekly reports on local tenant organisations such as the United Irish League compiled according to branch are often very informative.

For example, in a weekly edition of the *Leinster Leader* (22 January 1881) a wealth of information can be accumulated regarding local estates during the land war. It features reports of Land League meetings and resolutions passed at them from about thirty different branches in Kildare, King's County and Queen's County; a very substantial article on a Land League meeting held at Castletown, Queen's County, listing those officers in attendance from that county and surrounding counties and giving an almost verbatim report of everything that was said; an article on the refusal of Lord Mayo's Kildare tenants to pay their rents; a feature on a deputation of tenants who approached Lord Fitzwilliam at Coolattin for an abatement of rents, and a letter praising 'the usual and most liberal donation of clothing to the poor on the Drogheda estate' and the generosity of Lady Drogheda in supplying soup and food to '150 destitute persons'.

In order to locate relevant local newspapers, a researcher should consult James O'Toole's *Newsplan: Report of the newsplan project in Ireland* (Dublin, and

London, 1992) which provides a list of all newspapers held in the main public libraries in Ireland and in the British Library.[88] A full list of provincial newspapers for each county available in the National Library of Ireland may be consulted at the desk. Occasionally issues which are not available in the main repositories may be found in local libraries or may even be consulted in the newspaper's office (providing the newspaper is still in existence).

As with other sources newspapers have their strengths and weaknesses. A certain bias exists in all newspapers. At a national level, for example, the *Irish Times* had an obvious unionist bias in the nineteenth century, while the *Freeman's Journal* had nationalist tendencies. The same is often true of newspapers at local level. For example, the *Northern Standard* in County Monaghan had a unionist bias while the *Dundalk Democrat* served as its nationalist counterpart.[89] However, the value of having two such newspapers circulated in one county means that the researcher can view events and reactions to them from opposing perspectives. It is important to be aware of the identity of owners and editors of local newspapers and their politics. It might be interesting, for example, to compare reports on an eviction featured in two local newspapers which differ in their sympathies.

Newspapers of the early nineteenth century were selective in their coverage. If the researcher is aware of a significant event which occurred on an estate but finds no report of it in a local newspaper, this should not be regarded as proof that the event did not actually take place. An editor may not have wished to offend members of his readership. Similarly, early newspaper editors often relied on local landlords or their agents or local schoolteachers to supply them with some of their news items. The interests of such 'reporters' must be kept in mind. It was not until the late nineteenth century that newspapers increased in size and shorthand reporters were employed to cover local events. Subsequently, reports became more detailed and their verbatim-type reporting allows the researcher to be a little more discerning.

Unfortunately, few newspapers are indexed.[90] Therefore, researchers need to spend a lot of time searching through weekly editions of local newspapers which are perhaps best used for the study of an estate when one takes a particular topic over a relatively short period of time such as the Great Famine, or the land war 1881–84. The patience that is required to search through weekly editions will generally be rewarded with a vast and variable range of information of significance that may not be available from other sources.

XI. MISCELLANEOUS SOURCES

The foregoing sections have presented details regarding the main sources available for the study of the landed estate in Ireland. There are other sources available to help one complete the overall picture; the relevance of these depends on the focus of study.

The importance of estate maps has been discussed earlier in this section. Local historians are well advised to examine all the maps which they can find in order to locate and reconstruct the layout of the estate under study. In this respect the maps of the Ordnance Survey can be of significant help. The Ordnance Survey was established in the Phoenix Park, Dublin, in 1824, when a parliamentary committee of that year, investigating local taxation, advised that the whole of the country should be mapped in detail on the scale of six inches to the mile as a necessary prerequisite for valuing property and assessing tax liability. By 1846 this task had been completed and 1,906 sheets on the recommended scale had been compiled. These maps were subsequently used by Sir Richard Griffith in his valuation and later by the Irish Land Commission and the Congested Districts Board as they proceeded to break up Irish landed estates from the 1880s. J.H. Andrews points out that as the number of six inch sheets per county ranged from 25 to 153 (in the case of Cork), there was a need for separate index diagrams which in turn became important maps in their own right.[91] The index diagrams 'gave a surprisingly full if somewhat congested picture of roads, rivers, towns, villages, large houses and demesnes'.[92] Because the index diagrams delineate demesnes, it is easier for the historian to pin-point their actual location than it would be to take this information from the six-inch maps. As the early Ordnance Survey maps were compiled in the pre-Famine period they offer a unique insight into farming and settlement patterns.

In the post-1922 era, a separate Ordnance Survey office for Northern Ireland was established in Belfast and the records for the six counties were transferred there. The Ordnance Survey offices in the Phoenix Park, Dublin and Stranmillis Court, Belfast continue to house fine collections of records.[93] Besides their maps and letters, the records include information pertaining to the sale and break-up of estates such as rentals, statements of conditions of sale and descriptions of properties which may sometimes include a photograph of the big house on the estate. Ordnance Survey maps may also be consulted in other repositories such as the National Library or Trinity College Library.

For those interested in the level of indebtedness of Irish landlords in the second half of the nineteenth century, L.P. Curtis jr.'s article on this topic shows how the mortgage records of Maynooth College[94] and the Representative Body of the Church of Ireland[95] can be used to good effect.[96] In 1869, the Church of Ireland received £8.5 million in compensation under the Disestablishing Act of that year, while Maynooth College received £369,000. Both the finance committee of the Church of Ireland and the trustees of Maynooth College invested a substantial proportion of their capital in mortgages to Irish landowners at interest rates of usually 4.25 per cent.

The mortgage ledgers of the Representative Church Body show the amount of the various loans approved to landowners and one is able to identify the effects of agricultural depression and agitation from the early 1880s owing to the growth in interest arrears which are also recorded. When these ledgers are used in conjunction with the annual reports of the Representative Church Body one gains a good insight into the pressures on landlords to meet financial obligations at this time and on institutions to safeguard their investments.[97]

The importance of the Maynooth mortgage papers lies in the fact that they contain a great deal of correspondence between landlords and the college trustees from the early 1870s up to the early years of the twentieth century. These papers contain interesting information regarding the seven landowners who received loans including the initial loan agreements which usually set out the loan amount agreed upon; the rate of interest; the rate of penal interest in event of non-payment; the acreage and rental of the estate and the charges upon it. Also included are statements of interest accounts, private censuses of tenants on some estates (most notably on the Granard estate), details of the break-up and sales of estates, a revealing substantial volume of correspondence between landowners or their representatives throughout the country and the college trustees. This correspondence shows the human side of the story which statistics and accounts cannot do.[98]

For the late nineteenth century, a useful source is the confidential monthly collection of reports of the county inspectors of the Royal Irish Constabulary. These were part of the Colonial Office, Dublin Castle records.[99] They are mainly handwritten summaries of the main events in the county for each month of the year based on reports received by county inspectors from their district inspectors. The originals are available in the Public Record Office, London (CO 903–906) but they are also available on microfilm in the National Library of Ireland.[100] The content of the county inspectors' reports vary depending on the diligence of the individual officers and some can be quite illegible.[101] Most reports provide a good deal of information on estates on which agitation took place; details on significant land sales in the county during the month; and for the revolutionary period 1919–21, the difficulties facing landowners in each county as lawlessness grew and land grabbing became a way of life.

The revolutionary period of 1919–23 proved, in many cases, to be the final catalyst in the decline of estates. The political revolution was accompanied by a social revolution in the form of a new phase of land agitation. Section one has shown that many landowners had held on to extensive tracts of demesne and untenanted land (and, indeed, some retained much tenanted land) down to 1919. Because of their socio-political, economic and religious backgrounds landlords were to suffer outrage and intimidation from 1919 to 1923 on a scale the like of which their class had not experienced in living memory. This included the burning of around 300 big houses. Elements of this intimidation can be extracted from a study of local newspapers. However, much can also be gleaned from government files in the National Archives. The Department of the Taoiseach, Department of Finance, and Department of Justice files contain reports on individual estates during this period as well as correspondence between landlords and these various departments. For example, in September 1922 W.T. Cosgrave received a report from Lord Lansdowne's agent in Kerry which illustrates the type of pillaging that took place during the civil war:

> On arrival at Derreen the scene that greeted our eyes beggars description, crowds of every description around the house, men, women and children, pulling, hauling, fighting for what they could take. The house is absolutely destroyed, doors all smashed, every particle of furniture taken.[102]

Indexes to these files are to be found on the shelves in the National Archives. The index to the Department of Justice files lists those which are related to 'land' (H77/-) giving a brief description of what is to be found in individual files such as 'demesne land at Newberry manor, Mallow'; 'estate of T. Wilson Walshe: lands of Killowen, County Wexford'; 'payment of rents by tenants: W.S. Hugo, Glenwood, Rathdrum, County Wicklow'. The Department of Finance files, also indexed, relate mainly to land purchase on individual estates in the 1920s; arrears of annuities; and compensation being sought by landowners for loss of property. The Department of Taoiseach files mainly contain letters from landlords seeking protection from agitators during the revolutionary period. Here the index should be consulted under the headings of 'subjects', 'people' and 'places'. Even with the available indexes, much searching has to be done to ascertain if the government files contain anything on a specific estate, so the researcher should be prepared to spend some time going through them.

More information on the revolutionary period pertaining to compensation sought by landlords for damage to their estates and big houses can be found in the Damage to Property (Compensation) Act, 1923: Register of claims. This register is arranged on a provincial and county basis and is also available in the National Archives in the Office of Public Works files.[103] These files record the amount claimed in compensation under the 1923 act and indicate the final awards made. They also contain such information as reports of inspecting officers regarding the damage done to estates or big houses.[104]

Finally, census related material may be beneficial to those interested in a more specialised area of estate life such as the big house. Printed census reports for the nineteenth and early twentieth centuries can provide a general idea of the community in which the house or estate was located.[105] The 1851 report is particularly important as it shows the area, population, and number of houses by townland thereby enabling the researcher to compare the pre-Famine and post-Famine landscape.

Unfortunately, only the household schedule returns of the 1901 and 1911 censuses are extant. Some survive for the 1891 census, but none for an earlier census.[106] These household schedule returns (or census enumerators' books) were completed by the head of each household. For the 1901 and 1911 censuses two forms are especially useful when researching a landed estate. Form A constitutes 'a return of the members of the family and their visitors, boarders, servants, etc. who slept or abode in this house on the night of . . . '. It contains the names of those present with the name of the head of the family appearing first along with details of the relationship of the others present to the head of the family; their religion, their ability to read and write, age, rank, profession or occupation, marital status, where they were born and their ability to speak and or write Irish. The Form B completed by the enumerators, and attached to the household enumeration forms for their district, contains details on houses specifying the number of rooms in use, the number of windows and whether the house had a slated or other type of roof.

The household schedule returns for the twenty-six counties are available in the National Archives while those for the six-counties are in P.R.O.N.I. To locate the household schedule return of a big house, one simply needs to know the townland in which it was located. Often, this townland is specified as the demesne, for example, Charleville demesne, Castlesaunderson demesne etc. One then needs to consult the *Townland index* to find the D.E.D. number in which the townland was located. Indexes for each county are divided by D.E.D. with a reference number for the townland within the D.E.D. These two numbers and the name of the county are all that are required to procure the household schedule returns.

One can use both forms A and B to gather information on topics such as the actual size of the big house on an estate. However, one must be careful in relying on census data for while most returns probably give an accurate estimate of the number of rooms in a big house, other owners interpreted their instructions literally and gave merely the number of rooms 'in use'. One can access information on the number and type of outoffices attached to a big house. Similarly, information can be gathered on servants – the number employed, their religion and place of birth. One needs to be careful in this respect also for census returns show that many landlords were absent on the night on which the 1901 and 1911 forms were completed and therefore it is probable that many of their servants were with them and that what remained in many houses was merely a skeletal staff.

Researching landed estate records:
some problems and possibilities

INTRODUCTION

The study of a landed estate is a very challenging one. Indeed, the first challenge lies in locating the sources that can be used. The second and greater challenge stems from the complexities that can be involved in writing a study; two researchers may come to very different conclusions using the same set of estate records.[1] The aim of this section is firstly to alert the researcher to some of the problems which may be encountered during research, and secondly to explore some of the aspects of the history of landed estates which need more attention from historians

1. PROBLEMS

Sources must be approached in as unbiased a manner as possible. The perusal of a set of estate rentals may suggest to the researcher that all rents were extortionate, or that some tenants on the estate were being rackrented as their rents per acre were substantially higher than the valuation or those of fellow tenants on another part of the estate. To assess the real significance of rent levels, a number of factors need to be considered such as agricultural prices at the time, the size of the holding, the quality of the land, and the general ability of tenants to pay. As W.E. Vaughan observes regarding earlier studies of rent movements: 'How rents could be discussed without constant references to prices and production is a mystery, which must stand as one of the triumphs of faith over reason.'[2]

The same cautionary note applies to the study of the eviction question. Statistics do not offer reasons for evictions. When reasons are sought one may be surprised to find that what has previously been understood to be the causes, based perhaps on oral history or even biased newspaper reports, tells only part of the story. Landlords did not evict solely because tenants could not pay their rents. Estate records show that landlords did not generally press their tenants for rents during years of particular hardship. They tended to allow arrears to accumulate in the hope of recovering them during good years. Frequently evictions took place for a variety of other reasons unrelated to the payment of rents such as tenants sub-dividing their holdings against a landlord's wishes or practicing bad husbandry.[3]

Estate records should be used as correctives to other sources and, indeed, to ideas once or presently propounded on estate management. In 1950, K.H. Connell argued that landlords promoted subdivision in order to increase their rental income – a number of smaller holdings was more profitable than one larger one.[4] Estate records show, however, that landlords were largely unaware of what middlemen were doing. Certainly their apathy in not rectifying the situation earlier than they did can be criticised, but one must consider whether they had the power to do so if they wanted? Estate records can provide as much unwitting as intended testimony. While rentals clearly show the amount of rent which was paid each year, they also reveal much about arrears. It is possible to trace when arrears were most pronounced and if they coincided with periods of agricultural depression or widespread agitation. It is also possible to examine the effects that the growth in arrears or the granting of abatements had on landlords' net income.

It must also be emphasised that estate records are the most important sources in analysing the actual transformation of the estate area and the landscape as a whole. Even if a collection is fragmentary, other sources can be used to supplement the material contained in a collection to recreate an impression of the making, working and decline of an estate.[5] Estate maps, as pointed out in section two, are a most useful tool in this respect. Maps dating from the eighteenth and nineteenth centuries, particularly those produced by the French school of land-surveyors, are excellent starting points.[6] They can be used in conjunction with the Ordnance Survey's six-inch maps, the 1835 tithe applotment books, Griffith's valuation, the cancelled books and other estate records to trace the changes in the nineteenth-century landscape.

Estate valuations, leases, rentals, account books, and demesne farm account books all provide the data to allow the researcher to analyse changing patterns of landholding, rent movements and tenurial rights on an estate. Unwitting information such as the extent of tillage farming amongst a landlord's tenantry may perhaps be gauged from the amount of corn coming into a demesne as part payment of rents. Estate agents' letters or reports for their landlords and landlords' replies reveal most about estate administration and changing policies. The period from the late eighteenth century to the end of the Napoleonic wars was characterised by a high level of landlord investment in the elaboration of their estates – big houses were modified or built from scratch; demesnes were shaped; avenues and roads were constructed; new outoffices were built; existing cabins were swept away; gardens were made; large areas were planted with woodland.[7] In many cases, the natural environment was reshaped by professional designers.[8] Often, this involved a restructuring of landholdings: landlords sometimes acquired properties as leases fell in or relocated tenants to other parts of the estate in an attempt to augment their demesnes. Such information can be gleaned from appropriate estate records.

The elaboration of demesnes and building of big houses reflected landlord wealth in the period before the Napoleonic wars. This buoyancy may also be reflected in the growth of an estate's labour force. This should be clear from a study of estate employees account books. From these one can also recreate an image of the veritable hive of industry that existed inside demesne walls. Contracts signed between landlord and employees will not only reveal payments to employees but also perks, in the form of accommodation etc., which were available to estate employees such as lodgekeepers, stewards and bailiffs. It might be interesting to examine whether employees in positions of authority such as the steward, head gardener, head bailiff and others themselves leased farms from the landlord and if so, to investigate where these farms were located. Evidence for the Dartrey estate in Co Monaghan, for example, points to the fact that some landlords liked to have their demesne surrounded by farms leased to such employees. Further information on estate employees can be gleaned from the household schedule returns of the 1901 and 1911 censuses. An analysis of these can reveal much about landlord employment policy. One can examine if employees shared the same religion as their landlord employer, or if employees born in the locality were entrusted with positions of authority in the big house or on the estate.

At the beginning of the nineteenth century, in the aftermath of the Famine and from the early 1880s onwards, landlords appropriated tenanted lands and used them for their own farming purposes. The buoyancy in cattle prices from 1865 to 1883 and from 1900 to 1920, for example, led to an increase in farm sizes and the number of large graziers in the country. In the 1880s evictions had left landlords with vacant holdings which they retained for themselves. If they did not actually work this land, they tended to consolidate holdings into large farms to let to graziers on the eleven month system. The full extent of landlord involvement in large-scale farming or their utilisation of the eleven month system requires much work by historians. Information on such landlord policy can be gleaned from reports of various commissions.[9] The cancelled books in the Valuation Office should be examined to ascertain which vacated farms were converted by landlords into untenanted pasture. A parliamentary return of 1906 serves as a good indicator of the amount of untenanted lands in the hands of landlords at this time.[10] Again estate maps, surveys, and leases can provide further vital information.

Other sources such as newspapers and contemporary works must be approached with a degree of circumspection and even scepticism. While newspapers are a very important source for the study of any landed estate, the information contained in them should be cross checked with other sources whenever possible.

The same is true of other contemporary works which the researcher might consult to gain an understanding of issues affecting landed estates. Michael Davitt's *Fall of feudalism* (1904) may contain some important information on the Land League, its tactics and ideology, but Davitt's own background, his close involvement in the events of the time, and the fact that it was written some twenty years after the events had taken place should be borne in mind. His generalisation, for example, that landlords carried out the 'grossest acts of tyranny' with impunity does not stand up to scrutiny when applied to individual estates, for while there certainly were landlords who abused their powers, there were many more who used their powers benevolently.[11]

Likewise, it would be dangerous to perceive a landlord as 'good' or 'bad' based on a study of the level of rents on his estate.[12] A careful examination of rent increases, levels of evictions, responses to tenants' difficulties, and the character of the landlord himself (or his agent) is necessary to determine his true character.

By the same token, the study of a landed estate over a lengthy period must take into consideration the different landlords (and agents) who supervised its management. Each landlord had a different approach to administering the estate; inevitably estate management policy varied to at least some degree from one generation to the next for personal reasons, if not because of external factors dictating change. A number of witnesses to the Bessborough commission showed their awareness of this. Robert Reeves, a land agent in Limerick and Queen's County, claimed that 'a landlord today may be a good man, but his son may be a very different one, or he may be in good circumstances now, and may in a few years get into difficulties'.[13] John Gamble, a seed merchant from Derry, contrasted the notorious third earl of Leitrim with his father who Gamble claimed was 'considered one of the best landlords in the country' and 'indulgent as a landlord to an extraordinary degree'.[14]

A landed estate is a community in its own right which is as worthy of study as the community occupying a townland, parish or county. The study of individual estates is necessary to examine the fortunes of the landed class but while each estate should be studied on its own terms, one must take into account external factors which infringed upon estates in the nineteenth century. Estates were not static and just as they may have changed over time in response to internal forces such as a change of management policy by an heir, they also had to change in response to pressures from outside such as famine, agricultural depression, the growth in agrarian movements, the land war, the closing of mortgage facilities, and the pressures to sell land to occupying tenants exerted by mass movements such as the Land League, the National League and the United Irish League.

Wider economic changes had ramifications for all local estates. The agricultural depression in the 1880s, accompanied by the rise of the Land League, led to a decline in rents, a rise in landlord indebtedness and a growing acceptance amongst landlords that the sale of estates was inevitable. Allied to social and political change this brought a change in landlord-tenant relations. Regarding the typical Irish landlord in the late 1880s, the report of the

Cowper commission concluded that he had 'ceased to be the owner, and is placed more in the position of an encumbrancer on his property, in the improvement of which he no longer has any interest, while his influence for good has been much diminished'. With regard to landlord–tenant relations, the same report went on: 'The tenants as a rule, have not much regard for the landlords as such. In the north they are generally indifferent to them, and in the south they are often bitterly hostile'.[15] The establishment of the Free State after 1921 had further ramifications: the desire of the new government to appease the land-hungry and its desire to achieve social stability was a major influence in framing the terms of the 1923 Land Act which introduced compulsory acquisition. In summation, it is desirable for the local historian to take on board a wide range of historical dimensions – economic, social and political – when studying a landed estate, and by extension, the local historian must analyse as many sources as possible so as to document an estate's history as fully as he or she can.

The distinction which the report of the Cowper commission made between tenants in the north and in the south of the country highlights another complexity in the study of the Irish landed estate, that of regional variations. These variations do not simply apply to matters such as differences in soil or the type of farming practiced. The so called 'Ulster custom' may have existed in the south, but it did not predominate to the same extent as it did in the northern province. In Ulster, it is probably fair to conclude that landlord–tenant relations never reached the hostile levels of the south. Ulster had a much higher degree of industrialisation in the nineteenth century than the other three provinces. This helped alleviate the pressure on the land as labourers could find alternative employment in industry. Yet, even within Ulster there were regional variations. The farmers of south Monaghan and south Cavan had probably more in common with those of north Leinster than the rest of Ulster, while those in much of Donegal practiced subsistence farming on the same level as farmers in the western province of Connaught. As some landlords had property spread over different counties and provinces, these variations could be as marked for one landlord's estate as for the whole country. It is, therefore, necessary for the historian to be aware of the importance of geographical and topographical variations. Landscapes undoubtedly influenced the rental capacity of estates and the type of husbandry practiced in various parts of the country. The local historian should become acquainted with the setting of the estate by studying the local landscape.

Such variations within Ireland and between one estate and another have presented difficulties to historians – it is extremely difficult to make broad generalisations when they exist. In a national history it is not possible to assess the diversity and uniqueness of each estate in a general way: the history of each estate is much too complex to allow that. If and when enough studies of local estates have been completed, it will be easier to make more confident generalisations through comparative studies and thereby increase our knowledge and understanding of landlordism at a national level. Already the limited number of existing local studies have helped to reassess the traditional picture of the stereotypical rackrenting landlord and future studies can only act as correctives to the existing work of national historians or help to qualify the conclusions reached by them.

II. POSSIBILITIES

It is difficult to recreate the world of an Irish estate over the entire period from 1800 to the 1930s. To do so one would need access to a complete collection of estate records. Thus, some researchers may decide to study a particular aspect of estate life such as rent movements for which rentals are vital, or the sale of an estate under the various land acts which can be accomplished through a study of parliamentary papers. Others may choose to study several aspects of the landed estate during a particular period. For any chosen timescale, there is much work to be done. Little has been written of landed estates in the early part of the nineteenth century. Precise information on both the pattern of landholding structures and individual estates in this era is lacking. The Famine of the 1840s has been something of a focal point for historians studying landownership in nineteenth century Ireland, but the first four decades of the century should not merely be regarded as a prelude to the Famine as it is a period which is worthy of study in its own right. The Famine has been considered to be the primary reason for the population decline on estates but historians need to investigate the degree to which other structural changes in the economy, such as the collapse of local domestic industry, may have contributed to this decline.

There is plenty of scope for work on the effects of the Famine on individual estates. Questions such as – Did the famine change estate management policy? How did landlords react to the plight of their tenants? Did they grant abatements? Did they provide work relief? How did they react to their own financial crises? Were there evictions and clearances? Did the landlord manage to consolidate his holdings? – all need to be addressed. While new evidence suggests that there were many landlords who survived the Famine in a strong enough position to consolidate their own holdings through the purchase of property belonging to insolvent landowners, not enough is known about who these landowners were and how they had managed to remain solvent. Did those who used assisted emigration as a means of relieving distress do so for paternal reasons or were they motivated by a stronger desire to consolidate their holdings and, thereby, realise greater long term profits?

The period from the Famine to the beginning of the land war has, like the pre-Famine era, been largely neglected by historians in the past. Its importance in its own right has now been accepted, W.E. Vaughan's *Landlords and tenants in mid-Victorian Ireland* being testimony to this. However, little has appeared in print regarding individual estates during this time. It would, for example, be interesting to study the tenant farmers on individual estates who survived the Famine. They were undoubtedly relatively large farmers who in a short time after the Famine found their prosperity greatly increased. Questions which need to be addressed include the following: by the early 1880s, how actively involved were they or their successors in the Land League as memories of the Famine loomed large once again? How did their relationship with their landlords change from the post-Famine period to the land war? By the mid-1850s, were rents being paid in full and on time and were Famine arrears cleared? How was rental affected by temporary agricultural depression in the early 1860s? Was there a correlation between depression and a rise in evictions? What was the economic position of the estate during the boom years from the mid-1860s to the late-1870s? Did the landlord borrow heavily during these good years with serious consequences for the long term future of the estate? While valuable work has been done in this area by L.P. Curtis jr., much more remains to be done. It has been shown that tenant farmers certainly prospered during these decades, but was their prosperity in any way aided by the movement of landlords themselves into farming and their promotion of good farming habits amongst their tenants?

The economic boom ended rather abruptly in the late 1870s. The period of the land war has received a great deal of attention from historians: like the Famine in the middle of the century, it has proved to be a focal point. But much of this focus has been on the Land League, its composition and aims. The effects of the land war on individual estates has yet to be fully examined. Why did tenants on an estate react to this economic depression when they had not done so in the early 1860s? How did the Land League function on individual estates? How did the call for reductions or rent strikes affect the financial status of the estate? There is evidence to suggest, for example, that tenants who supposedly supported rent strikes paid their rents secretly. During the troubled years of the mid-1880s when the Plan of Campaign was initiated on his estate, Lord Granard wrote to his mortgagees, the trustees of Maynooth College, informing them that he was not receiving any rents from his tenants. However, it transpired in a court hearing in 1888, that he had, in fact, been receiving rental income above his rent roll.

Much work remains to be done on the operation of the Plan of Campaign on individual estates. We know that it was put into effect on around 200 estates,[16] but how did the initiation of the Plan of Campaign on a local estate impact on neighbouring estates? When landlords found their estates under threat from the Land League or the National League, how did they react? Similarly more information is needed on the United Irish League of 1898–1902 (and, indeed, its resurgence in certain areas during World War I). What part did it play in the break up of estates in the early nineteenth century? Indeed, the whole impact of the various land acts on estates needs to be examined.

Little has appeared in print about the history of estates after 1903. The Wyndham Land Act of that year did not end landlordism in Ireland. Many landlords continued to retain substantial untenanted land and some retained substantial tracts of tenanted land for many years after. These landlords came under great pressure after 1919 with the outbreak of a new land war. However, little is known of their plight. Many questions need to be answered here. How many landed estates survived up to 1923? How were they affected by the events of the revolutionary period, 1919–23? The sale of these estates under the 1923 and succeeding Free State Land Acts needs to be examined. It is certain that landlords who sold under these acts did so under much more unfavourable terms than had been available twenty years before under the Wyndham Land Act. Not only were they forced to sell for a fixed price of fifteen years' purchase on current rents, they were also paid in land bonds instead of cash.

Conclusion

There is no doubting the fact that since the 1970s much valuable work has been done by historians to foster an understanding of the system of landlordism in Ireland in the nineteenth and early twentieth centuries. However, much remains to be done. It is only through the study of local landed estates that this task can be accomplished. To date too few of them have been studied in their own right. The study of more estates can only encourage comparative studies and expose the anomalies that existed from one estate to another and act as correctives to national histories which, because of their very nature, tend to hide such anomalies in generalisations.

Notes

INTRODUCTION

1 Raymond Gillespie and Gerard Moran, 'Land, politics and religion in Longford since 1600' in Raymond Gillespie and Gerard Moran (ed.), *Longford: essays in county history* (Dublin, 1991), p. 7.
2 See J.E. Pomfret, *The struggle for land in Ireland, 1800–1923* (Princeton, N.J., 1930), pp 26–8; K.H. Connell, 'The land legislation and Irish social life' in *Economic History Review*, xi (1958), pp 1–7.
3 W.A. Maguire, *The Downshire estates in Ireland, 1801–45* (Oxford, 1972); R.B. MacCarthy, *The Trinity College estates, 1800–1923: corporate management in an age of reform* (Dundalk, 1992): W.J. Lowe, 'Landlord and tenant on the estates of Trinity College, Dublin, 1851–1903' in *Hermathena*, cxx (1976), pp 5–24; Lindsay Proudfoot, 'The management of a great estate: patronage, income and expenditure on the duke of Devonshire's Irish property, c.1816–91' in *Irish Economic and Social History*, xiii (1986), pp 32–55; Olive Robinson, 'The London companies as progressive landlords in nineteenth-century Ireland' in *Economic History Review*, 2nd ser., xv, 1 (Aug. 1962), pp 103–18.
4 W.E. Vaughan, *Landlords and tenants in mid-Victorian Ireland* (Oxford, 1994); J.S. Donnelly jr., *The land and people of nineteenth century Cork: the rural economy and the land question* (London, 1975); B.S. Solow, *The land question and the Irish economy, 1870–1903* (Cambridge, Mass., 1971).
5 Raymond Gillespie and Gerard Moran, 'Introduction: writing local history' in Raymond Gillespie and Gerard Moran (ed.), *'A various country': essays in Mayo history, 1500–1900* (Westport, 1987), p. 22.

CHAPTER ONE

1 R.B. MacCarthy, *The Trinity College estates, 1800–1923: corporate management in an age of reform* (Dundalk, 1992); Lowe, 'Landlord and tenant on the estates of Trinity College'; Robinson, 'The London companies as progressive landlords in nineteenth-century Ireland'; idem., 'The London companies and tenant right in nineteenth-century Ireland', in *Agricultural History Review* xviii (1970), pp 54–63.
2 For the management of an absentee estate, see J.S. Donnelly jr., 'The journal of Sir John Benn-Walsh relating to the management of his Irish estate, 1823–64' in *Cork Historical Society Journal* cxxix (1974), pp 86–123; cxxx (1975), pp 15–42; For a study of absenteeism in Co Monaghan in mid-nineteenth century, see P.J. Duffy, 'Irish landholding structures and population in the mid-nineteenth century' in *Maynooth Review*, iii (1977), p. 18.
3 *Return for the year 1870, of the number of landed proprietors in each county, classed according to residence, showing the extent of land held by each class . . .* H.C. 1872 (167), xlvii. 782.
4 Samuel Clark, *Social origins of the Irish land war* (Princeton, 1979).
5 For memoirs of nineteenth-century land agents see S.M. Hussey, *The reminiscences of an Irish land agent* (London, 1904); W.S. Trench, *Realities of Irish life* (London, 1868). For functions and social backgrounds of agents see J.S. Donnelly jr., *Land and people of nineteenth-century Cork*, pp 173–87; Maguire, *The Downshire estates*, pp 155–205.
6 J.S. Donnelly jr points out that 'estate agents in nineteenth-century Ireland enjoyed a much greater measure of autonomy in the management of landed property than did their

64

counterparts in England'. Donnelly, *Land and people of Cork*, p. 173.

7 David Dickson, 'Middlemen' in Thomas Bartlett, and D.W. Hayton (ed.), *Penal era and golden age: essays in Irish history* (Belfast, 1979), pp 162–85; G.E. Christianson, 'Landlords and land tenure in Ireland, 1790–1830' in *Éire-Ireland*, ix (1974), pp 25–58.

8 For rent movements at this time see, David Large, 'The wealth of the greater Irish landowners, 1750–1815', in *Irish Historical Studies*, xv (1966), pp 21–47; also Peter Roebuck, 'Rent movement, proprietorial incomes, and agricultural developments, 1730–1830' in Peter Roebuck (ed.), *Plantation to partition: essays in Ulster history in honour of J.L. McCracken*, (Belfast, 1981) pp 82–101.

9 *Report from her majesty's commissioners of enquiry into the state of the law and practice in respect to the occupation of land in Ireland. Minutes of evidence*, pt. ii [616], HC 1845, xx. 1.

10 J.J. Lee, *The modernisation of Irish society, 1848–1918* (Dublin, 1973), p. 2; see also W.E. Vaughan and E.J. Fitzpatrick (ed.), *Irish historical statistics: population, 1821–1971* (Dublin, 1978); Duffy, 'Irish landholding structures', pp 3–27.

11 Samuel Clark and J.S. Donnelly jr. (ed.), *Irish peasants: violence and political unrest, 1780–1914* (Wisconsin and Manchester, 1983), pp 30–31; P. O'Donoghue, 'Causes of the opposition to tithes, 1830–38' in *Studia Hibernica*, no. 5 (1965), pp 7–28; idem, 'Opposition to tithe payments in 1830–31' in *Studia Hibernica*, no. 6 (1966), pp 69–98; idem, 'Opposition to tithe payments in 1832–33' in *Studia Hibernica*, no. 12 (1972), pp 77–108.

12 P.E.W. Roberts, 'Caravats and Shanavests: Whiteboyism and faction fighting in East Munster, 1802–11' in Clark and Donnelly, *Irish peasants*, pp 64–101.

13 For a contemporary study of Irish agrarian crime see G.C. Lewis, *On local disturbances in Ireland, and on the Irish church question* (London, 1836); for more recent studies see M.R. Beames, *Peasants and power: the Whiteboy movements and*

their control in pre-Famine Ireland (Brighton, 1983); W.G. Broehl, *The Molly Maguires* (Cambridge, Mass., 1964); J.S. Donnelly jr., 'The Rightboy movement, 1785–8' in *Studia Hibernica*, nos 17–18 (1977–78), pp 120–202; idem, 'The Whiteboy movement, 1761–5' in *Irish Historical Studies*, xxi, no. 81 (Mar. 1978), pp 20–54; idem, 'Pastorini and Captain Rock: Millenarianism and sectarianism in the Rockite movement of 1821–4' in Donnelly and Clark (ed.), *Irish peasants*, pp 102–39; T.D. Williams (ed.), *Secret societies in Ireland* (Dublin and New York, 1973); Tom Garvin, 'Defenders, Ribbonmen and others: underground political networks in pre-famine Ireland' in *Past and Present*, no. 96 (1982), pp 133–55.

14 For rent movements before the Famine see Donnelly, *Land and people of Cork*, pp 48–53 and Maguire, *The Downshire estates*, pp 28–64.

15 Donnelly, *Land and people of Cork*, p. 49.

16 Vaughan, *Landlords and tenants in mid-Victorian Ireland*, pp 24–26. For local studies of estates during the Famine see, Patrick Feeney, 'Balysaggart estate: eviction, famine and conspiracy' in *Decies*, no. 27 (Autumn, 1984), pp 4–12; Eileen McCourt, 'The management of the Farnham estates during the nineteenth century' in *Breifne*, iv (1975), pp 531–60; for more general studies on the effects of famine on estate management, see relevant chapters of Donnelly, *Land and people of Cork*; L.M. Cullen, *An economic history of Ireland since 1660* (London, 1972); R.D. Edwards and T.D. Williams, *The Great Famine: studies in Irish history, 1845–52* (New York, 1957); J.M. Goldstrom, 'Irish agriculture and the Great Famine' in J.M. Goldstrom and L.A. Clarkson (ed.), *Irish population, economy and society: essays in honour of the late K.H. Connell* (Oxford, 1981), pp 155–71; Cormac Ó Gráda, *Ireland before and after the Famine: explorations in economic history, 1800–1925* (Manchester, 1988); T.P. O'Neill, 'The Irish land question, 1830–50' in *Studies*, xliv (Autumn, 1955), pp 325–36.

17 Donnelly, *Land and people of Cork*, pp 71–2.
18 12 & 13 Vict., c. lxvii (28 July 1849).
19 Later the Landed Estates Court and later still the Land Judges Court.
20 See Mary Lyons, *Illustrated Encumbered Estates Ireland, 1850–1905* (Whitegate, Clare, 1993).
21 See P.G. Lane, 'The Encumbered Estates Court, Ireland, 1848–49' in *Economic and Social Review*, iii (1972), pp 413–53; idem, 'The general impact of the Encumbered Estates Act of 1849 on Counties Galway and Mayo' in *Galway Archaeological and Historical Society Journal*, xxxiii (1972–3), pp 44–74; idem, 'The impact of the Encumbered Estates Court upon the landlords of Galway and Mayo' in *Galway Archaeological and Historical Society Journal*, xxxviii (1981–2), pp 45–58.
22 J.S.Donnelly jr., *Landlord and tenant in nineteenth-century Ireland* (Dublin, 1973), p. 49. Twenty-five years' purchase of current rents means the yearly rental of the property sold multiplied by twenty-five. The up-turn in Irish agriculture from the mid-1850s led to a dramatic decline in the number of petitions presented in the 1860s and the early 1870s. The Landed Estates Court was wound-up in 1879.
23 See Vaughan, *Landlords and tenants in mid-Victorian Ireland* and Donnelly, *Land and people of Cork*. See also Solow, *The land question and the Irish economy;* Paul Bew, *Land and the national question in Ireland, 1858–82* (Dublin, 1978); J.S. Donnelly jr., 'The Irish agricultural depression of 1859–64' in *Irish Economic and Social History*, iii (1976), pp 33–54; W.E.Vaughan, 'Landlord and tenant relations between the Famine and the land war', in L.M. Cullen and T.C. Smout (ed.), *Comparative aspects of Scottish and Irish economic and social history, 1600–1900* (Edinburgh, 1977), pp 216–26; idem, 'Agricultural output, rents and wages in Ireland, 1850–80' in L.M. Cullen and F. Furet (ed.), *Ireland and France, 17th–20th centuries: towards a comparative study of rural history* (Paris, 1990), pp 85–97; idem, 'An assessment of the economic performance of Irish

landlords, 1851–81' in F.S.L. Lyons and R.A.J. Hawkins (ed.), *Ireland under the union: varieties of tension: essays in honour of T.W. Moody* (Oxford, 1980), pp 173–99; P.G. Lane, 'The management of estates by financial corporations in Ireland after the Famine' in *Studia Hibernica*, no. 14 (1974), pp 67–89; T.P. O'Neill, 'From Famine to near famine, 1845–79' in *Studia Hibernica*, no. 1 (1961), pp 161–71.
24 Donnelly, *Land and people of Cork*, pp 182–5.
25 D.S. Jones, *Graziers, land reform and political conflict in Ireland* (Washington, 1995), pp 121–23.
26 Cormac Ó'Gráda, 'The investment behaviour of Irish landlord, 1850–75: some preliminary findings' in *Agricultural History Review*, xxiii (1975), pp 151–3. On nine estates, W.E. Vaughan estimates that the average was probably no more than 4 or 5 per cent. See Vaughan, *Landlords and tenants in mid-Victorian Ireland*, pp 122–3, 277–8.
27 The fact that the cottier and small-holding classes had been largely wiped out by the Famine undoubtedly curtailed agrarian agitation.
28 See Vaughan, *Landlords and tenants in mid-Victorian Ireland*, pp 20–26; idem, *Sin, sheep and Scotsmen: John George Adair and the Derryveagh evictions, 1861* (Belfast, 1983); also Gerard Moran, *The Mayo evictions of 1860: Patrick Lavelle and the 'war' in Partry* (Cathair na Mart, 1986).
29 Vaughan, *Landlords and tenants in mid-Victorian Ireland*, pp 138–60; David Fitzpatrick, 'Class, family and rural unrest in nineteenth-century Ireland' in P.J. Drudy (ed.), *Irish studies 2, Ireland: land, people and politics* (Cambridge, 1982), pp 37–75; Charles Townshend, *Political violence in Ireland: government and resistance since 1848* (Oxford, 1983), pp 14–24; A.C. Murray, 'Agrarian violence and nationalism in nineteenth-century Ireland: the myth of Ribbonism' in *Irish Economic and Social History*, xxiii (1986), pp 56–73. For local agrarianism between the Famine and land war see Brendan Mac Giolla Choille, 'Fenians, Rice and Ribbonmen in County

Monaghan, 1864–67' in *Clogher Record*,
vi, 2 (1967), pp 221–52; Kevin
MacMahon and Thomas McKeown,
'Agrarian disturbances around
Crossmaglen, 1835–55' in *Seanchas
Ardmhacha*, ix, 2 (1979), pp 302–32; x,
1 (1981), pp 149–75; x, 2 (1982),
pp 380–416; J.W. Hurst, 'Disturbed
Tipperary 1831–60' in *Éire-Ireland*, ix
(1974), pp 44–59.

30 Donnelly, *Landlords and tenants in
nineteenth-century Ireland*, p. 60.

31 For a contemporary insight to Irish
land laws see A.G. Richey, *The Irish
land laws* (London, 1880).

32 Vaughan, *Landlords and tenants in mid-
Victorian Ireland*, p. 71. For a full
discussion on tenant-right see ibid.,
pp 67–102.

33 T.A.M. Dooley, 'The decline of Carton
house and estate, 1870–1950' in *Journal
of the Kildare Archaeological Society*, xviii,
2 (1994–5), p. 218.

34 W.E. Vaughan has pointed out that
rents collected between 1851 and 1880
amounted to £354 million; if they had
kept abreast of agricultural output the
total would have been £400 million,
or 13 per cent more. See Vaughan,
*Landlords and tenants in mid-Victorian
Ireland*, p. 21.

35 Ibid., p. 48; Donnelly, *Land and people of
Cork*, pp 191–4; Solow, *The land
question*, pp 66–70; T.A.M. Dooley, 'The
decline of the big house in Ireland,
1879–1950' (unpublished Ph.D thesis,
N.U.I. Maynooth, 1996), pp 102–3.

36 See Vaughan, *Landlords and tenants in
mid-Victorian Ireland*, pp 208–16;
Donnelly, *Land and people of Cork*,
p. 249ff; Samuel Clark, *Social origins of
the Irish land war* (Princeton, NJ, 1979);
idem, 'The social composition of the
Land League' in *Irish Historical Studies*,
xvii, 68 (Sept. 1971), pp 447–79; A.W.
Orridge, 'Who supported the land
war? an aggregate-data analysis of Irish
agrarian discontent, 1879–82' in
Economic and Social Review, xii, 3 (April,
1981), pp 203–33; Bew, *Land and the
national question in Ireland*; idem, 'The
Land League ideal: achievement and
contradictions', in Drudy (ed.), *Irish
studies, 2. Ireland: Land, politics and*

people, pp 77–92; W.L. Feingold, *The
revolt of the tenantry: the transformation of
local government in Ireland, 1872–86*
(Boston, 1984); idem, 'Land League
power: the Tralee poor-law election of
1881' in Clark and Donnelly (ed.), *Irish
peasants*, pp 285–310; R.W. Kirkpatrick,
'Origins and development of the land
war in mid-Ulster' in Lyons and
Hawkins (ed.), *Ireland under the union*,
pp 201–35; Gerard Moran, 'An
assessment of the Land League
meeting at Westport, 8 June 1879' in
Cathair na Mart, iii, 1 (1983), pp 54–9;
idem, 'Famine and the land war: relief
and distress in Mayo, 1879–81', in ibid,
v, 1 (1985), pp 54–66; vi, 1 (1986), pp
111–27; idem, 'James Daly and the rise
and fall of the Land League in the
west' in *Irish Historical Studies*, xxix,
no. 114 (Nov. 1994), pp 189–97;
Desmond Murphy, 'The land war in
Donegal, 1879–91' in *Donegal Annual*,
xxxii (1980), pp 476–86; Francis
Thompson, 'The landed classes, the
Orange Order and the anti-Land
League campaign in Ulster, 1880–81'
in *Éire-Ireland*, xxii, 1 (Spring, 1987), pp
102–21; J.W.H. Carter, *The land war and
its leaders in Queen's County, 1879–82*
(Portlaoise, 1994).

37 W.E. Vaughan, 'Richard Griffith and
the tenement valuation' in G.L.H.
Davies and R.C. Mollan (ed.), *Richard
Griffith, 1784–1878: papers presented at the
centenary symposium organised by the
Royal Dublin Society, 21 and 22 Sept.
1978* (Dublin, 1980), pp 103–22.

38 See, L.P. Curtis jnr., 'Incumbered
wealth: landed indebtedness in post-
Famine Ireland' in *American Historical
Review* lxxxv, 2 (Apr. 1980), pp 332–67;
Vaughan, *Landlords and tenants in mid-
Victorian Ireland*, pp 130–37.

39 *A return showing according to provinces
and counties the number of cases in which
judicial rents have been fixed by all the
matters provided by the Land Law Acts for
a first and second statutory term respectively
to 31 December 1902 with particulars as to
acreage, former rents of holdings, and percentage of reductions in rents*. HC 1903, lvii.
91. See also K.L. Buckley, 'The fixing
of fair rents by agreement in County

Galway, 1881–5 in *Irish Historical Studies*, vii, 27 (Mar. 1959), pp 149–79.

40 Laurence Geary, *The Plan of Campaign, 1886–91* (Cork, 1986), p. 180.

41 45 & 46 Vict., c.xlix (18 Aug. 1882), and *Return of payments made to landlords by the Irish Land Commission pursuant to the first and sixteenth sections of the Arrears of Rent (Ireland) Act 1882*. HC 1884, lxiv, 97.

42 David Cannadine, *The decline and fall of the British aristocracy* (Yale, 1990), p. 95.

43 Fixity of tenure was given to a tenant as long as he paid his rent and observed his covenant; the aforementioned fair rent proviso was established; and a tenant was allowed free sale of his interest in his holding. For an excellent analysis of the mechanics of the Land Acts from 1881 to 1923 see, J.T. Sheehan, 'Land purchase policy in Ireland, 1917–23: from the Irish Convention to the 1923 Land Act' (Unpublished M.A. thesis, NUI Maynooth, 1993). See also, C.F. Kolbert and T. O'Brien, *Land reform in Ireland: a legal history of the Irish land problem and its settlement* (Cambridge, 1975); K.H. Connell, 'The land legislation and Irish social life' in *Economic History Review* 2nd ser. xi, 1 (Aug. 1958), pp 1–7; Clive Dewey, 'Celtic agrarian legislation and Celtic revival: historicist implications of Gladstone's Irish and Scottish Land Acts, 1870–86' in *Past & Present*, no. 64 (Aug. 1974), pp 30–70. Also of value L.P. Curtis jr., *Coercion and conciliation, 1880–92: a study in Conservative Unionism* (Princeton, 1963); Alan Gailey, *Ireland and the death of kindness: the experience of Constructive Unionism, 1890–1905* (Cork, 1987); W.J. Winstanley, *Ireland and the land question, 1800–1922* (London, 1984).

44 The annuity was the tenant purchaser's annual repayment on the loan.

45 *A return showing as far as practicable for each year the lowest and highest prices (in each calendar year) of guaranteed land stock and the number and amounts of loans under the Land Purchase (Ireland) Acts 1891 and 1896*. HC 1903, lvii. [Hereafter *Return of land stock, 1903*].

46 *Report of the Estates Commissioners for the year from 1 April 1920 to 31 March 1921 and for the period from 1 November 1903 to 31 March 1921* HC 1921, xiv.

47 *Return of land stock, 1903*.

48 For the case of Sir Henry Gore Booth, see *Report of the royal commission on the Land Law (Ireland) Act, 1881, and the Purchase of Land (Ireland) Act, 1885*. [C4969], HC 1887, xxvi, 1, p. 473.

49 This was a landlord organisation set up in 1886 because landlords felt they needed to protect their interests and property from the threat posed by the National League, the Plan of Campaign, and government legislation which they perceived to be infringing upon their tenurial rights.

50 *Return of the resolution and statement adopted by the Irish Landowners Convention on 10 Oct. 1902 . . . HC*, 1903, lvii, 321.

51 For a more indepth discussion on the workings of the 1903 Land Act see L. Paul-Dubois, *Contemporary Ireland* (English translation, London, 1908), pp 282–9.

52 The 1909 Land Act reverted to the old system of payment by land stock. For the experience of Co Cavan landowner, Col. Edward Saunderson, see Alvin Jackson, *Col. Edward Saunderson: land and loyalty in Victorian Ireland* (Oxford, 1995).

53 *Report of the Estates Commissioners for the year from 1 April 1920 to 31 March 1921 and for the period from 1 November 1903 to 31 March 1921*. HC, 1921, xiv.

54 W.L. Micks, *An account of the Congested Districts Board for Ireland, 1891–1923* (Dublin, 1925).

55 *Royal commission on congestion in Ireland: Final report*. [Cd 4097] HC, 1908, xlii, pp 12–13.

56 *Irish Land Commission report for the period from 1 April 1923 to 31 March 1928*, p. 20.

57 A return for 1906 calculated that there was approximately 2.6 million acres of untenanted land in Ireland at that time. *Return of untenanted lands in rural districts, distinguishing demesnes on which there is a mansion, showing: rural districts and electoral divisions; townland; area in statute acres; poor law valuation; names of occupiers as in valuation lists*. HC, 1906, c.177.

58 *Report of Estates Commissioners . . . to 31 March 1921* [Cmd 1150], HC, 1921, xiv, 661.

59 *Morning Post*, 17 Feb. 1903.

60 See *Royal commission on congestion in Ireland: Appendix to tenth report, minutes of evidence taken in Counties Galway and Roscommon, 18 September to 4 October 1907 and documents relating thereto.* [Cd 4007], HC 1908, xliii, p. 117.

61 The highest bidder secured the use of the land for an eleven month period, after which it went up for auction once again. The advantages of this system to the landlord were that the occupier could not claim formal tenancy and thereby could not avail of the rent fixing terms of the 1881 Land Act and occupiers could be evicted without notice to quit.

62 D.S. Jones, 'The cleavage between graziers and peasants in the land struggle, 1890–1910' in Clark and Donnelly, *Irish peasants*, pp 374–413; idem., *Graziers, land reform and political conflict in Ireland* (Washington, 1995).

63 By June 1901, there were 1,000 branches of the U.I.L. with an estimated membership of 100,000 throughout the country. See F.S.L. Lyons, *John Dillon* (London, 1968); Paul Bew, *Conflict and conciliation in Ireland, 1890–1910: Parnellites and radical agrarians* (Oxford, 1987); J.V. O'Brien, *William O'Brien and the course of Irish politics, 1881–1918* (London, 1976).

64 County inspector's confidential monthly reports, Co Galway, 1905–14 (P.R.O., CO 904).

65 For an insight see, Arthur Mitchell, *Revolutionary government in Ireland: Dail Eireann 1919–22*, (Dublin, 1995), pp 130–36.

66 Memo. by Patrick Hogan on 1922 land bill, 14 Dec. 1922 (N.A.I, Dept. of Taoiseach files, S1955).

67 Patrick Hogan to William Cosgrave, 7 April 1923 (N.A.I., Dept. of Taoiseach files, S3192).

68 These were defined as farms 'used for the convenience of the owner's residence . . . and not merely as an ordinary farm for the purpose of profit'.

69 *Dail debates*, xlviii, 13 July 1933, 2378–95.

70 *Irish Land Act 1933, no. 38 of 1933*, section (29).

71 Kolbert and O'Brien, *Land reform in Ireland*, p. 55.

CHAPTER TWO

1 Lewis, *Topographical dictionary*, p. 9.

2 Information of this type can also be taken from Lewis's *Topographical dictionary*.

3 Works acquired after 1968 are listed in a separate card catalogue in the N.L.I.

4 Rosemary ffolliott and D.F. Begley, 'Guide to Irish directories' in D.F. Begley (ed.), *Irish genealogy: A record finder* (Dublin, 1981), pp 75–106.

5 National Library of Ireland, Kildare Street, Dublin 2.

6 Some of the abbreviations in *Hayes's catalogue* are now out of date, for example the S[tate] P[aper] O[ffice] and the P[ublic] R[ecord] O[ffice] have been amalgamated to form the National Archives. Occasionally one may find a reference such as F 59 (1–24). These usually refer to manuscript maps, or valuation surveys with maps which are kept on microfilm in the N.L.I.

7 Public Record Office Northern Ireland, 66 Balmoral Ave., Belfast BT9 6NY.

8 National Archives, Bishop Street, Dublin 8.

9 Trinity College Dublin, Library, College Street, Dublin 2. T.K. Abbott, *Catalogue of manuscripts in the library of Trinity College Dublin* (London, 1908) catalogues accessions up to 1900. The catalogue is continued after that date in typescript form.

10 One possible means of identifying the estate's solicitors is to consult the Land Commission papers pertaining to the estate. However, these are not always easily accessed.

11 Clonbrock estate rent ledger, 1881 (N.L.I., Clonbrock papers, MS 19,634).

12 Clonbrock estate account book, 1868 (N.L.I., Clonbrock papers, MS 19,511).

13 See for example, Dunmore farm account books, 1883–94 (N.L.I., Ormonde papers, MS 23,833).

14 For the case of the duke of Leinster
   Irish Times, 28 Dec. 1880.
15 For secondary sources on maps, see:
   Paul Ferguson, *Irish map history: A select
   bibliography of secondary works, 1850–
   1983, on the history of cartography in
   Ireland* (Dublin, 1983); J.H. Andrews,
   *Plantation acres: an historical study of the
   Irish land surveyor and his maps* (Belfast,
   1985); idem, *Shapes of Ireland: maps and
   their makers, 1564–1839* (Dublin, 1997);
   idem, *History in the Ordnance map, an
   introduction for Irish readers* (2nd ed.,
   Kerry, Montgomeryshire, 1993).
16 See J.H. Andrews, 'The French school
   of Dublin land surveyors' in *Irish
   Geography*, v, no. 4 (1967).
17 Survey of Lord Cloncurry's Kildare
   estate, 1838 (N.L.I., Cloncurry papers,
   MS 5,667).
18 James Edward Vaughan's surveys of
   Lord Clonbrock's estate, 1832 (N.L.I.,
   Clonbrock papers, MSS 22,008–09).
19 There is also an index of maps available in the N.L.I. that can be consulted
   in the reading room. Many of these
   maps are of estates in the nineteenth
   century. However, 'for urgent
   conservation reasons' some of these
   maps may not be available for
   consultation.
20 Lord Ormonde's agent to Michael
   Donovan, 25 Jan. 1883 (N.L.I.,
   Ormonde letter books, MS 23,580).
21 Lord Ormonde's agent to Thomas
   Kennedy, 9 May 1884 (ibid.).
22 Farnham estate correspondence, 1898
   (N.L.I., Farnham papers, MS 18,618).
23 Fitzwilliam ejectment books, 1845–60;
   1861–86 (N.L.I., Fitzwilliam papers,
   MSS 4972, 4992).
24 Of the thirty-one sets of estate records
   found by Donnelly relating to Co
   Cork, only nine were in public
   repositories. Donnelly, *Land and people
   of Cork*, pp 386–7.
25 Excellent use has been made of
   existing records by W.J. Smyth to trace
   the making of the estate landscape.
   W.J. Smyth, 'Estate records and the
   making of the Irish landscape: an
   example from County Tipperary' in
   Irish Geography, ix (1976), pp 29–49.
26 Donnelly, *Land and people of Cork*, p. 8.

27 There are few estate collections as
   comprehensive in scope for the
   nineteenth century and early twentieth
   century as the Ormonde or Clonbrock
   collections in the N.L.I. or the
   Downshire collection in P.R.O.N.I..
28 Vaughan, *Landlords and tenants in mid-
   Victorian Ireland*, p. 277. Similarly, estate
   accounts will not necessarily reveal the
   full extent of a landlord's indebtedness.
   Lord Ormonde's personal overdraft for
   the 1890s does not appear in estate
   accounts but his auditor's reports refer
   to its dangerously high level on a number of occasions (N.L.I., Ormonde
   papers, MSS 23,725–26).
29 See J.H. Johnson, 'The Irish tithe
   composition applotment books as a
   geographical source', in *Irish Geography*
   xi (1958), pp 254–61; R.C. Simington,
   'The tithe composition applotment
   books', in *Analecta Hibernica*, no. 10
   (July 1941), pp 295–8.
30 The N.L.I. index to tithe applotment
   books is divided into counties and
   parishes within each county are then
   listed alphabetically. The parish name,
   diocese, county, date of valuation, tithe
   applotment book reference, and
   microfilm number is given.
31 There are no books for fifteen parishes
   in the twenty-six counties, eleven of
   these being Dublin parishes.
32 For the setting up of the valuation and
   the relationship of the valuation to the
   real letting value of land see Solow, *The
   land question*, pp 59–67. See also W.E.
   Vaughan, 'Richard Griffith and the
   tenement valuation' in G.L.H. Davies
   and R.C. Mollan (ed.), *Richard Griffith,
   1784–1847* (Dublin, 1980), pp 103–22.
33 The call number is Ir 3335 g10.
34 Valuation Office, Irish Life Centre,
   Abbey Street, Dublin.
35 See J.S. Donnelly jr., *Landlords and
   tenants in nineteenth-century Ireland*
   (Dublin, 1973), pp 9–10.
36 Hugh Shearman, 'The citation of
   British and Irish parliamentary papers
   of the nineteenth and twentieth
   centuries' in *Irish Historical Studies*, iv,
   13 (Mar. 1944), p. 33.
37 See also P. and G. Ford's *A guide to
   parliamentary papers: what they are, how to*

find them, how to use them (Oxford, 1955); A. and J. Maltby, *Ireland in the nineteenth century: a breviate of official pubications* (Oxford, 1979); P. & G. Ford, *Select list of British parliamentary papers, 1833–1899* (Oxford, 1953) reprinted Shannon, 1969; P. & G. Ford, *A breviate of parliamentary papers, 1900–1916* (Oxford, 1957); idem, *A breviate of parliamentary papers, 1917–39* (Oxford, 1951). For the post-1922 period, see idem, *A select list of reports and inquiries of the Irish Dail and Senate, 1922–72* (Dublin, 1974); A. Maltby and B. McKenna, *Irish official publications: A guide to Republic of Ireland papers with a breviate of reports, 1922–72* (Oxford, 1979); A. Maltby, *The government of Northern Ireland, 1922–72: a catalogue and breviate of parliamentary papers* (Dublin, 1974).

38 See for example the excellent lists of parliamentary papers in Donnelly, *Land and people of Cork*, pp 393–404; Vaughan, *Landlords and tenants in mid-Victorian Ireland*, pp 294–309.

39 B.L. Solow, *The land question and the Irish economy, 1870–1903* (Cambridge, Mass., 1971).

40 The life of a select committee usually lasted just one parliamentary session; a commission usually had a much longer period of time to carry out its inquiry.

41 *Report from her majesty's commissioners of inquiry into the state of the law and practice in respect to the occupation of land in Ireland* [605], HC 1845, xix. 1; *Minutes of evidence, pt.i* [606], H.C. 1845, xix. 57; *Minutes of evidence, pt. ii* [616], HC 1845, xx.1; *Minutes of evidence, pt. iii* [657], HC 1845, xxi.1; *Appendix to minutes of evidence, pt. iv* [672], HC 1845, xxii. 1; *Index to minutes of evidence, pt. v* [673], H.C. 1845, xxii. 225.

42 *Report of her majesty's commission of enquiry into the working of the Landlord and Tenant (Ireland) Act 1870 and the Acts amending the same* [C2779], HC 1881, xviii; *Minutes of evidence, part I* [C2779], HC 1881, xviii, 73; *Minutes of evidence and appendices, part ii* [C2779], HC 1881, xix, I; *Index to minutes of evidence and appendices* [C2779], HC 1881, xix, 825.

43 *Report of the royal commission on the Land Law (Ireland) Act 1881 and the Purchase of Land (Ireland) Act 1885* [C4969], HC 1887, xxvi, I; *Minutes of evidence and appendices* [C4969], HC 1887, xxvi, 25; *Index to evidence and appendices* [C4969], HC 1887, xxvi, 1109.

44 For example *Report from the select committee on Irish Land Act 1870; together with the proceedings of the committee, minutes of evidence, appendix and index* HC 1877 (388), xii, 1 (George Shaw Lefevre, Chairman).

45 Besides the report and minutes of evidence of the enquiry into these evictions, the names of the tenants evicted were also published in a parliamentary paper. *Report from the select committee on Kilrush Union; together with proceedings of the committee, minutes of evidence, appendix and index* HC 1850 (613), xi. 529; *Report and returns relating to evictions in the Kilrush Union* [1089], HC 1849, xlix, 315.

46 *First report from his majesty's commissioners for enquiring into the condition of the poorer classes in Ireland, with appendix (A) and supplement,* HC 1835 (369), xxxii, pt I, 1; *Second report of the commissioners for enquiring into the condition of the poorer classes in Ireland* [68], HC 1837, xxxi, 587.

47 *Preliminary report from her majesty's commissioners on agriculture* [C2778], HC 1881, xv, 1; *Minutes of evidence, pt* 1, H.C. 1881, xv.1; *Digest and appendix to minutes of evidence, pt. I, with reports of assistant commissioners* [C2778–II], HC 1881, xvi,1; *Minutes of evidence, pt.ii,* [C3069], HC 1881, xvii, 1; *Minutes of evidence, pt. iii* [C3309–I], HC 1882, xiv, 45; *Digest and appendix to minutes of evidence, pts. ii and iiii,* ibid., [C3309–II], 493; *Preliminary report of the assistant commissioners for Ireland* [C2951], HC 1881, xvi, 841; *Final report from her majesty's commissioners on agriculture* [C3309], HC 1882, xiv, 1.

48 In total there were eleven reports between 1906 and 1908. The reference for the first report is as follows: *First report of the royal commission appointed to enquire into and report upon the operation of the acts dealing with congestion in Ireland* [Cd 3266], HC 1906, xxxii, 617; *Evidence and documents* [Cd 3267], HC 1906, xxii, 621.

49 See for example, V.G. Kiernan, 'The emergence of a nation' in C.H.E. Philpin (ed.), *Nationalism and popular protest in Ireland* (Cambridge, 1987), p. 30.

50 Vaughan, *Landlords and tenants in mid-Victorian Ireland*, p. 44.

51 *Return of untenanted lands in rural districts, distinguishing demesnes on which there is a mansion, showing: rural district and electoral divisions; townland; area in statute acres; poor law valuation; names of occupiers as in valuation lists.* HC 1906, c.177.

52 *Number of estates offered for sale, and withdrawn for want of purchasers, in the court of the commissioners of Incumbered Estates in Ireland, stating owners, counties, denominations of land, rental and price offered; and number of estates sold, stating rental, amount, and date of sale and payment, date of distribution of money to creditors, and interest borne thereon, if not distributed.* HC 1850 (757), li.491; *Estates in Ireland on which the quit and crown rents were purchased by the commissioners for the sale of Incumbered Estates in Ireland; specifying the rate of purchase of such quit rents; and also the number of years purchase at which such estates were sold, calculated on the rental of estates when held by proprietors; and the charges subject to which such estates were sold up to 22 July 1851.* HC 1851 (602), l. 875. See also *Report of the commissioners for the sale of Incumbered Estates as to their progress etc.* HC [1268], xxv.55 and HC 1851 (258), xxiv. 35.

53 *Return of payments made to landlords by the Irish Land Commission, pursuant to the 1st and 16th sections of the [Arrears of Rent] Act; and also a return of rent charges cancelled pursuant to the 15th section of the act* [C4059], HC 1884, lxiv, 97.

54 *Return of estates purchased by the Congested Districts Board for Ireland in respect of the period of six months ended 30 April 1904, for the purpose of resale to tenants and the enlargement of holdings.* HC 1904, lxxx, 525.

55 *Return showing by counties the average number of years' purchase under the different Land Purchase Acts or clauses from 1870 to 1903, with the average percentage of reductions, the number and acreage*

of holdings purchased under each act and the amount of interest and sinking fund payable by the tenant purchasers . . . up to 1 November 1908 HC 1908, xc, 1413.

56 Details of sales and purchases under earlier acts are also available in parliamentary papers. See *Return of holdings purchased by tenants, and by other than occupying tenants, from the Church Temporalities (Ireland) Commissioners, specifying name of purchaser; benefice and denomination of land sold; county and barony; date of sale; acreage; valuation; annual rent; purchase money; gross amount; paid in cash; similar return of holdings purchased by tenants under the Land Acts 1870 and 1872 (excluding Church Temporalities land); of arrears due on above advances and on land not yet sold by the Church Commissioners.* HC 1880 (408), lvi. 707.

57 See for example, *General index to the bills, reports and papers printed by order of the House of Commons and to the reports and papers presented by command 1900–49,* p. 400–01.

58 Under different land acts, these columns varied.

59 See K.L. Buckley, 'The Irish Land Commission as a source of historical evidence' in *Irish Historical Studies*, viii (1952), pp 28–36.

60 Irish Land Commission, Records Branch, National Archives Building, Bishop Street, Dublin 8.

61 Keane's survey deals with the records accumulated by the Land Commission under the land acts from 1881 to 1909 inclusive. 8,447 boxes containing records relating to 9,343 estates were examined. However, it was really only the documents relating to title that were the principal subject of the survey.

62 Buckley, 'Land Commission records', p. 30. Documents for each estate have letters prefixed to denote the act under which the estate was purchased. 'L.C.' denotes 1881 Land Act; 'E.C.' denotes the 1903 and 1909 Land Acts; 'S' denotes the 1923 Land Act; 'C.D.B.' denotes that the sale took place under the auspices of the Congested Districts Board.

63 Buckley, 'Land Commission records', p. 35.

64 It should be noted here that the return of advances gives the relevant information regarding the poor law valuation of a holding, rent, and purchase price.

65 The latter two methods of fixing fair rents were quite common but once fixed the agreement was registered with the Land Commission.

66 Buckley, 'Land Commission records', p. 31.

67 The N.L.I. reference number for these reports of inspectors is P8383. See also Congested Districts Board, *Instructions and suggestions for the guidance of parish committees* (Dublin, 1911); idem, *List of electoral divisions that are congested in accordance with sect. 36 of the statute 54 & 55 Vict., c.48. 15* (Dublin, 1892). The minutes of the board are also available in the N.L.I.

68 See for example, *First annual report of the Congested Districts Board for Ireland for 1892* [Cd 6908] HC 1893–94, lxxi, 25.

69 For example, *First report of the royal commission appointed to enquire into and report upon the operation of the acts dealing with congestion in Ireland.* [Cd 3266] HC 1906, xxxii, 617: *Evidence and documents* [Cd 3267] HC 1906, xxii, 621.

70 Property which on the death intestate of the owner devolved on the heir.

71 Registry of Deeds, Henrietta Street, Dublin 1.

72 For introduction to the Registry of Deeds, see Peter Roebuck, 'The Irish Registry of Deeds' in *Irish Historical Studies*, xviii, no. 69 (Mar. 1972), pp 61–73.

73 A jointure was a provision made by a husband for the support of his wife after his death i.e. an annual income during widowhood.

74 This is a deed recording a transfer of property.

75 In the Landed Estates Court, unencumbered or marginally encumbered estates could be sold.

76 In P.R.O.N.I., there is a very valuable index to the Encumbered Estates Court sales. The reference number is MIC.80/2.

77 These were originally stored in the Public Record Office in 1881 on the instruction of Peter O'Brien, later lord chief justice of Ireland.

78 For the case of Lord Portarlington who almost bankrupted his estate as a result of his lavish expenditure on Emo Park, see Encumbered Estates Commission, *Report of the proceedings in the matter of the Portarlington estate* (Dublin, 1850).

79 It should be noted that some estate collections, such as the Leslie papers in the N.L.I., contain memoirs and diaries that have not been published in full or published at all.

80 This is true of works such as Lord Castletown, *Ego* (London, 1923); Earl of Dunraven, *Past times and pastimes* (2 vols, London, n.d.); Lord Dunsany, *Patches of sunlight* (London, 1938); Elizabeth, Countess Fingall, *Seventy years young* (London, 1937); Lord Rossmore, *Things I can tell* (London, 1912); Duc de Stacpoole, *Irish and other memories* (London, 1922).

81 Lady Gregory (ed.), *Sir William Gregory, K.C.M.G., formerly member of parliament and sometimes governor of Ceylon: an autobiography* (London, 1894).

82 For an opposite viewpoint of the Land League, see Michael Davitt, *The fall of feudalism in Ireland: or the story of the Land League revolution* (London and New York, 1904). For a 'personal narrative' of the land war see, W.S. Blunt, *The land war in Ireland, being a personal narrative of events* (London, 1912). See also B.H. Becker, *Disturbed Ireland: being the letters written during the winter of 1880–81* (London, 1881). For contemporary account of the land acts, see R.C. Cherry, *The Irish land law and Land Purchase Acts 1881, 1885, and 1887* (Dublin, 1888); A.G. Richey, *The Irish land laws* (London, 1880). On the Encumbered Estates Court, see P.H. Fitzgerald, *The story of the Encumbered Estates Court in Ireland* (London, 1862); J.P. Prendergast, *Letters to the earl of*

Bantry, or a warning to English purchasers of the perils of the Irish Encumbered Estates Court, exemplified in the purchase by Lord Charles Pelham Clinton M.P., of two estates in the barony of Bere, County of Cork (Dublin, 1854).

83 See for example information on Fitzwilliam estate, Dun, *Landlords and tenants*, pp 30–42.

84 Also of value is F.B. Head, *A fortnight in Ireland* (London, 1852); M.A. Titmarsh, *The Irish sketch book* (London, 1842); and Alexis De Tocqueville (J.P. Mayer, ed.), *Journeys to England and Ireland c.1835* (London, 1958).

85 See W.J. Sinclair, *Irish peasant proprietors: facts and misrepresentations* (London, 1880), p. 3.

86 Dun, *Landlords and tenants*, p. 25.

87 A forthcoming publication from Four Courts Press by Mary-Lou Legg, *Newspapers and nationalism: Irish provincial papers, 1850–92* should prove valuable.

88 Newspapers are listed according to title and they are cross-referenced according to county. Details regarding the run of newspapers are given as are details on where they are to be found in hard-copy or if they are available on microfilm. For other valuable works on newspapers in Ireland, see J.R.R. Adams, *Northern Ireland newspapers: checklist with locations* (Belfast, 1979); Ffoliott, 'Newspapers as a genealogical source' in Begley (ed.), *Irish genealogy: a record finder*, pp 117–38; Noel Kissane, *The past from the press* (Dublin, 1985); H. Oram, *The newspaper book: A history of newspapers in Ireland, 1649–1983* (Dublin, 1983).

89 Although printed in County Louth, this newspaper was widely circulated in County Monaghan.

90 The *Leinster Leader* indexation project, set up in September 1988, was the first of its kind in the Republic of Ireland. Its objective of indexing 110 years of the newspaper is nearing completion. See Mary Carroll, '*Leinster Leader* indexation project', in *Journal of Kildare Archaeological Society*, xviii, pt ii, pp 259–62.

91 See J.H. Andrews, *History in the ordnance map, an introduction for Irish readers* (2nd ed., Kerry, Montgomeryshire, 1993).

92 Ibid., p. 22.

93 Ordnance Survey Office, Phoenix Park, Dublin 8. Ordnance Survey of Northern Ireland, Colby House, Stranmillis Court, Belfast BT9 5BJ.

94 These records are stored in the Russell Library, Maynooth Campus, Co Kildare. Permission to consult these records should firstly be obtained from the Russell librarian.

95 Permission to consult these records should be sought through the Archivist of the Representative Church Body Library, Braemor Park, Rathgar, Dublin 14.

96 L.P. Curtis jr., 'Encumbered wealth: Landlord indebtedness in post-famine Ireland' in *American Historical Review*, lxxxv, 2 (Apr. 1980), pp 332–67.

97 These may be consulted in the N.L.I..

98 The mortgage papers should be used in conjunction with the *annual reports* of the president which are also available in the Maynooth archives. Other primary sources which are useful in this respect include the *Irish Landowners' Convention annual reports, 1887–1919* available in the N.L.I.

99 For a valuable introduction to these records, see the bibliography of David Fitzpatrick, *Politics and Irish life, 1913–21: provincial experience of war and revolution* (Dublin, 1977).

100 There is an index of the colonial office papers available at the desk of the N.L.I. CO904, parts ii–iv are composed of the county inspectors' monthly reports from 1892 to 1921.

101 These monthly reports were in turn summarised by the inspector general of the R.I.C. for the chief secretary.

102 Report enclosed in Lord Lansdowne to Winston Churchill, 20 Sept. 1922 (forwarded by Churchill to W.T. Cosgrave, 22 Sept. 1922) (N.A.I., Dept. of Taoiseach files, S/1940).

103 These are held in the Four Courts, so at least twenty-four hours notice should be given to the staff of the N.A.I. before consulting them.

104 Copy of report of Mr J.C. Butler, inspecting officer, on damage to Mitchelstown castle for the office of public works, 14 Aug. 1925 (N.A.I., Office of Public Works files, 2D/62/76). The Public Record Office, London contains the Irish compensation claims registers and indexes for 1922–30 in the Colonial Office papers (CO 905). Also, in R.B. McDowell's *The fate of southern Unionists: crisis and decline* (Dublin, 1997), the author has made extensive use of the criminal injuries – Irish Grants Committee – records, 1922–30 (P.R.O., CO 762) to illustrate the plight of southern Unionists (many of whom were landowners) in the early 1920s.

105 See Vaughan and Fitzpatrick (ed.), *Irish historical statistics: population, 1821–1971* (Dublin, 1978). Also very useful are Brenda Collins, 'The analysis of census returns: the 1901 census of Ireland' in *Ulster Local Studies*, xv, no. 1 (1993), pp 38–46; Rosemary ffolliott, 'Irish census returns and census substitutes' in D.F. Begley (ed.), *Irish genealogy: a record finder* (Dublin, 1987); S.A. Boyle, 'Irish manuscript census records: a neglected source of information' in *Irish Geography*, ii (1978), pp 110–25.

106 The household schedule returns for 1861, 1871, 1881 and 1891 were destroyed by government order. Those for 1821, 1831, 1841, 1851 were almost entirely destroyed in the fire at the Four Courts in 1922. Information on those that survived may be found in J.G. Ryan, *Irish records: sources for family and local history* (Salt Lake City, 1988).

CHAPTER THREE

1 Lindsay Proudfoot and J.S. Donnelly jr., for example, have reached different conclusions regarding management policy on the Devonshire estate in the nineteenth century. See Proudfoot, 'The management of a great estate', p. 33.

2 Vaughan, *Landlords and tenants in mid-Victorian Ireland*, p. 53.

3 See ibid., p. 29.

4 K.H. Connell, *The population of Ireland, 1740–1845* (Oxford, 1950).

5 See, Smyth, 'Estate records and the making of an Irish landscape'.

6 See J.H. Andrews, 'The French school of Dublin land-surveyors' in *Irish Geography*, iv (1967), pp 275–92.

7 Much information on the embellishment of demesnes and houses can be found in J.P. Neale, *Views of the seats of noblemen and gentlemen in England, Wales and Scotland and Ireland* (London, 1820).

8 See A.A. Horner, 'Carton, Co Kildare – a case study of the making of an Irish demesne' in *Quarterly Bulletin Irish Georgian Society*, xviii (1975), pp 45–103.

9 See for example, *Report from the select committee on Land Acts (Ireland), together with the proceedings of the committee, minutes of evidence, appendix and index*, H.C. 1894 (310), xiii; *Royal commission of inquiry into the procedure and practice and the methods of valuation followed by the Land Commission, the Land Judges' Court, and the Civil Bill Courts in Ireland under the land acts and the land purchase acts, report* [C 8734], H.C. 1898, xxxv, 1; *vol. ii: minutes of evidence* [C 8859], H.C. 1898, xxxv, 41; *First report of the royal commission appointed to enquire into and report upon the operation of the acts dealing with congestion in Ireland* [Cd 3266], H.C. 1906, xxxii, 617. *Evidence and documents* [Cd 3267], H.C. 1906, xxii, 621. (There are eleven reports in all with evidence and documents. *Digest of evidence* [Cd 4099], H.C. 1908, xliii, 369)

10 *A return of untenanted lands in rural districts* . . . H.C. 1906 (250), c.177.

11 Michael Davitt, *The fall of feudalism in Ireland: or the story of the Land League revolution* (London and New York, 1904), p. 142.

12 Solow, *The land question*, p. 43.

13 *Bessborough commission, minutes of evidence*, vol. i, p. 77.

14 ibid., p. 307.

15 *Cowper commission report*, pp 9–10.

16 For a list of these estates, see Geary, *The Plan of Campaign*, pp 154–78.